BFI Modern Classics

Rob White
Series Editor

Advancing into its second century, the cinema is now a mature art form with an established list of classics. But contemporary cinema is so subject to every shift in fashion regarding aesthetics, morals and ideas that judgments on the true worth of recent films are liable to be risky and controversial; yet they are essential if we want to know where the cinema is going and what it can achieve.

As part of the British Film Institute's commitment to the promotion and evaluation of contemporary cinema, and in conjunction with the influential BFI Film Classics series, BFI Modern Classics is a series of books devoted to individual films of recent years. Distinguished film critics, scholars and novelists explore the production and reception of their chosen films in the context of an argument about the film's importance. Insightful, considered, often impassioned, these elegant, beautifully illustrated books will set the agenda for debates about what matters in modern cinema.

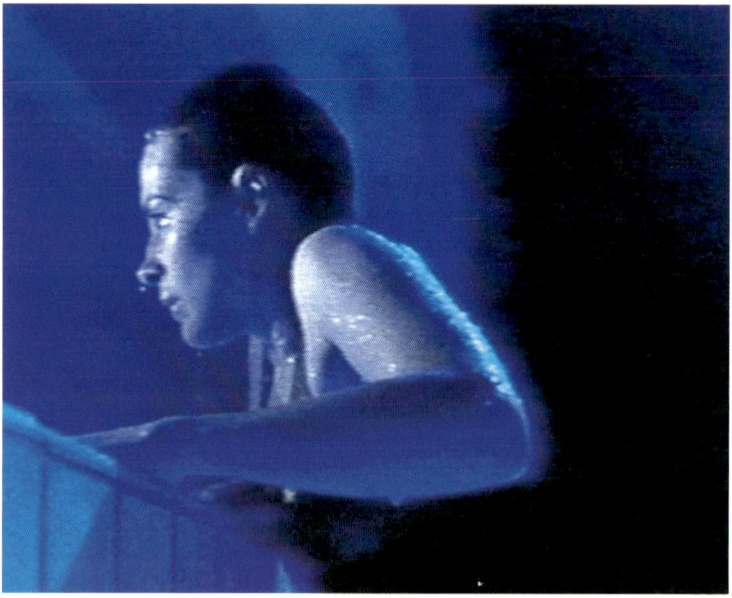

The
'Three Colours' Trilogy

Geoff Andrew

bfi Publishing

First published in 1998 by the
British Film Institute
21 Stephen Street, London W1P 2LN

Copyright © Geoff Andrew 1998
Reprinted 1999

The British Film Institute is the UK national agency with responsibility for encouraging the arts of film and television and conserving them in the national interest.

Series design by Andrew Barron &
Collis Clements Associates

Picture editing by Liz Heasman

Typeset in Italian Garamond
by D R Bungay Associates, Burghfield, Berks

Printed in Great Britain by
Norwich Colour Print, Drayton, Norfolk

British Library Cataloguing-in-Publication Data
A catalogue record for this book is available from the British Library.
ISBN 0-85170-569-3

Contents

Acknowledgments *7*

Introduction: Interpreting the Trilogy *9*

1 Before the Trilogy *12*

2 Making the Trilogy *21*

3 *Three Colours*: *Blue* *25*

4 *Three Colours*: *White* *38*

5 *Three Colours*: *Red* *52*

6 The Trilogy: Connections *67*

7 The Trilogy: Reflections *73*

8 The Trilogy: Coda *77*

9 Elegy: Remembering Kieślowski *81*

Notes *88*

Credits *90*

Bibliography *96*

Acknowledgments

The opinions expressed in this book are my own; no one else should be held responsible for them. Nevertheless, the text, as ever, is partly the result of a great deal of informal discussion over a long period of time with many people – too many, indeed, to thank individually. I hope they know who they are and accept my gratitude.

    I should, however, specifically like to thank Derek Adams, Brian Case, Wally Hammond, Trevor Johnston, Geoffrey Macnab, and most especially Tom Charity – all *Time Out* colleagues – for making my work on this book a little easier than it might otherwise have been. Thanks, also, to my parents, for their patience throughout; to Jane Hoodless, for her encouragement in the book's early stages; to David Meeker and Peter Wollen, who both suggested long ago that I contribute to the BFI Film Classics series; to Ed Buscombe, who commissioned and edited the book, for his understanding, expertise and advice; to Richard Paterson, for helping to see it through to completion; to Mark Sanderson, for his perceptive insights into *Blue* and all-round support; to Matthew Tempest, for sending me, unsolicited, his notes on the parallels between *Red* and *The Tempest*; to Artificial Eye and Sarah Harvey, for arranging my interviews with Krzysztof Kieślowski and for tapes of *The Decalogue* and the *Three Colours* trilogy; to Tony Rayns for first alerting me to Kieślowski's genius and for lending me tapes of *Blind Chance* and *No End*; to Danusia Stok, for translation during my meetings with Kieślowski; to Juliette Binoche, Julie Delpy and, especially, Irène Jacob for their comments on working with Kieślowski; and, last but in no way least, to the late director himself, for his friendly, lucid, thoughtful responses to my questions, and for the films he gave us.

    Finally, I should like to thank, and dedicate this book to, Alejandra de la Paz, without whom … .

AUTHOR'S NOTE
Though technically French–Polish–Swiss co-productions, the *Three Colours* films were officially titled in French as *Trois Couleurs: Bleu*, *Trois*

Couleurs: Blanc and *Trois Couleurs: Rouge*. For the sake of convenience and brevity, however, and because they were also widely known, even at their festival premieres, by their English titles, I refer to the individual films throughout the text as, respectively, *Blue*, *White* and *Red*, and to the series as the *Three Colours* trilogy.

Where Kieślowski himself is quoted, unless stated otherwise, the material derives from two interviews I myself conducted in London. All other quotations derive from Danusia Stok's book, *Kieślowski on Kieślowski* (see Bibliography). Any dialogue quoted from the films is from the versions sub-titled in English by Andrew Litvak and (in the case of *White*) Michael Smith, released on videocassettes by Artificial Eye.

Introduction: Interpreting the Trilogy

When on 13 March 1996 I first heard that Krzysztof Kieślowski had just died from a heart attack during a by-pass operation, I was surprised, upset, and a little stunned by the sense of strange coincidence, a twist of fate, as it were, that could have figured in one of his films. Only two days earlier, I had been listening to my tape recordings of his voice describing his plans to lead 'a normal life' after announcing his retirement from film-making. As soon as I'd recovered from the shock, and phoned the bad news to a number of friends who had also met him, I put aside the feature I was writing for *Time Out*, and immediately embarked instead on an obituary for the Polish director, in which among other things, I described my feeling that Kieślowski was, in some strange way, a friend, not because I'd had the good fortune to meet him a couple of times, but because his films had touched me in a profoundly personal way. And, I later discovered, I was not alone in this sensation; over the next few weeks I received a number of very gratifying letters from readers saying they felt exactly the same.

    Kieślowski, I think, would have been pleased by their reaction; after all, his stated reason for making films was to touch people, to make contact with them. As he told Danusia Stok for her excellent book of interviews *Kieślowski on Kieślowski*: 'The audiences I like most are those who say that the film's about them, or those who say that it meant something to them, those for whom the film changed something. … There aren't many of them but perhaps there are a few.'[1] Certainly, I count myself among that number (and perhaps they aren't so very few), which is one reason I decided to write this book – as a way of saying 'thank you' for the films Kieślowski gave us.

    I make no apologies, then, for the personal nature of these opening words, and indeed of much of what follows; movies, inevitably, provoke personal responses in the people who watch them – cinema, like music or painting, works on audiences in a very subjective way, particularly when it deals with 'inner lives' – and this was Kieślowski's avowed purpose. And yet towards the end of his life, as his films reached ever larger audiences, some critics complained that his work was becoming simultaneously too obscure and too polished; that his recent 'international' work was less satisfying than his earlier Polish films. Even some of his admirers took the view that the *Three Colours* trilogy was somehow beyond interpretation. Yet, if that were so, how did *Blue*, *White* and *Red* achieve their extraordinary success, not only winning major festival awards, but attracting large, very appreciative audiences? Clearly, they *did* make sense, *did* mean something to the vast majority of those

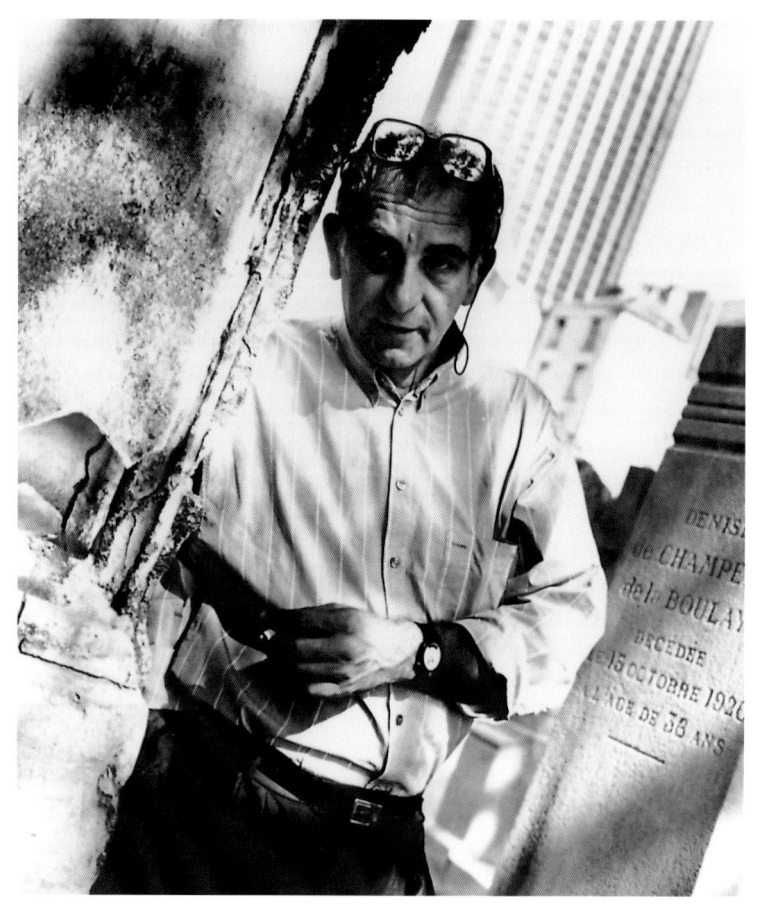

The late Krzysztof Kieślowski

who saw them. (Perhaps Kieślowski was rather more attuned to how audiences 'read' a film than many of his critics; though his later films often deal with the 'irrational' subject matter of emotional and spiritual lives, they do so – as I hope to show – in a thoroughly rational manner.) It is the purpose of this book to attempt to discover the 'meaning' of the *Three Colours* trilogy, and to examine the ways in which its creator tried to express that meaning.

This is not intended as a definitive account of *Blue, White* and *Red*. Rather, it reflects an unrepentant admirer's attempts to fathom the films' artistry, to explain as rationally as possible how they managed to affect him on a deeply emotional level. (This is not always an easy task in the case of Kieślowski; when I stumbled out of the Cannes première of *Red*, I was literally trembling and speechless for almost thirty minutes!) As such, the book has little time for facts and figures surrounding the films' making; there was little that was extraordinary about their production, and besides it is what the films 'say' and how they 'say' it, rather than the production costs, technical tricks or personalities involved, that make them interesting. Nor have I attempted an especially detailed contextualisation of the films politically or historically; their maker, long tired of politics, was insistent that his examination of the French Revolutionary ideals of Liberty, Equality and Fraternity should be understood in a personal, determinedly apolitical sense. What follows, then, is for want of a better description an 'auteurist' study; while, like Kieślowski himself, I am well aware that film-making is a collaborative art-form, circumscribed by economic, political, historical and cultural factors, my concern is to try to understand Kieślowski the artist at a particular point in his career. Since he was not a hack director-for-hire working for the Hollywood conveyer belt but a film-maker who by his own admission had enjoyed a great deal of artistic freedom and initiated all his own major projects, such an approach seems, to me at least, both justifiable and appropriate.

1 Before the Trilogy

Krzysztof Kieślowski was born in Warsaw in June 1941, the beginning of an unsettled childhood, not only because of the war and its aftermath but because his father suffered from tuberculosis, forcing the family to travel from one sanatorium town to another. Krzysztof sometimes changed school several times a year, but he performed well academically, though he found school of little value. Because he too had poor lungs, he spent a lot of time at home reading, and it was through books, he later claimed, that he realised 'there was something more to life than material things which you can touch or buy in shops'.[2]

At the age of sixteen, Kieślowski trained for three months as a fireman, but, partly to avoid military service, he returned to his studies at Warsaw's College for Theatre Technicians, where he fell in love with the theatre. Since it was impossible to become a stage director without qualifications in higher education, he then applied to the Łodz Film School; only on his third attempt did he succeed, by which time he was no longer interested in pursuing a theatrical career. Nevertheless, he enjoyed his four years at Łodz, watching and discussing films, and making both features and documentaries.

It was during this period that Kieślowski developed an interest in politics; in 1968, just before graduating, he took part in a student strike. Such activities, however, were hardly uncommon at that time, especially in Poland, where from 1968 onwards the Communist Party steadily reversed the slow, tentative progress towards greater personal, public and artistic freedom that had begun under Wladyslaw Gomulka. The post-'68 period of civil unrest, food shortages and widespread disillusionment, resulted in the rise of an uncensored underground press and 'The Flying University', which held lectures, discussions and other cultural gatherings in private houses; it was also a time when documentaries achieved an unprecedented popularity, purporting to show the realities of life as experienced by ordinary Poles, as opposed to the falsifications of Party propaganda. On graduating from film school, therefore, it seemed natural to Kieślowski to begin his professional film-making career as a documentarist.

Given the pervasive presence of politics in Polish life under the repressive Edward Gierek, it was perhaps inevitable that many of Kieślowski's documentaries concerned people working for, or fighting against, State institutions: *Factory* (*Fabryka*, 1970) alternated scenes of workers at the Ursus tractor factory with a management board meeting about the plant's inability to meet its production quota; *Workers '71* (*Robotnicy '71*, 1972) was an attempt 'to portray the workers' state of mind'[3] after the strikes of 1970 and the downfall of Gomulka; *Hospital* (*Szpital*, 1976) charted the determination of orthopaedic surgeons on a 32-hour shift to overcome dismal working conditions; and *From a Night Porter's Point of View* (*Z Punktu Widzenia Nocnego Portiera*, 1977) was a portrait of a fanatically right-wing, disciplinarian factory porter. Despite, however, the often controversial nature of Kieślowski's subject matter and approach (which resulted in some of his films being shelved for years) and the fact that in the late 1970s he became involved, as vice-president to Andrzej Wajda, in the struggles of the Polish Film-Makers' Association for greater artistic freedom ('We were completely insignificant,' he told Danusia Stok),[4] Kieślowski later insisted that his documentaries had been intended not as examinations of repressive political institutions but as portraits of individuals made from a humanistic point of view.

And indeed, there is some justification for this claim. While *From a Night Porter's Point of View* does, through its gentle mockery of the porter's extreme, conservative views on crime, punishment and authority, have clear social, political and ethical implications, it is at the same time primarily a (surprisingly sympathetic) character study of a rather sad and unfulfilled man. Likewise, if *Talking Heads* (*Gadające Głowy*, 1980), which asks seventy-nine Poles when they were born, what they do, and what they would most like, offers tantalising insights into the nature of contemporary Polish society, it also, by moving in quick linear fashion from the youngest to the oldest interviewee, becomes a universally applicable essay on the emotional, physical and psychological effects of ageing. One senses that, even at this stage in his career, whatever interest Kieślowski had in the world of politics derived largely from his fascination with its effects upon the individual. Increasingly, however, he came to feel that this fundamentally humanist fascination was ill served by documentary: the very process of making documentaries, because it invaded people's privacy, prevented him from getting as close to the heart of personal experience as he wanted, while actors, in fiction film, might allow him greater access to the realm of people's inner lives.

After General Wojciech Jaruzelski's clampdown on the free trade union Solidarity and the introduction of martial law in December 1981, Kieślowski seems to have become increasingly disillusioned with politics. By this time, he had virtually abandoned documentary work for fiction features, achieving his first international success with *Camera Buff* (*Amator*, 1979), a droll satire in which a man's progress from shooting home-movies of his family to making documentaries about and for the factory where he works brings him into conflict with his censorious bosses. Clearly, there was more than a hint of political comment here, as

'What if …?': *Blind Chance*, a film in the conditional mood

there would be in *Blind Chance (Przypadek,* 1981), in which a medical student runs to catch a train, with three potentially different outcomes: he catches it, falls in with a Communist and becomes a Party activist (resulting in his betrayal of a girlfriend); he crashes into a station guard who, by having him arrested and brought to trial, inadvertently drives him to join the militant underground; or he misses it, bumps into a lover he later marries, completes his studies with considerable success, ignores politics and finally, sent abroad on a trip that is the crowning point of his career to date, dies in a plane crash. Again, the various options of political life in Poland determine the film's subject matter, although Kieślowski himself saw it as 'no longer a description of the outside world but rather of the inner world'.[5] Certainly, it's impossible to ignore certain crucial, non-political, philosophical elements – crossed wires, interwoven lives, the mysterious, cruelly ironic workings of fate and chance, the narrative's 'conditional' mood of 'what if?', all which occur, with increasing frequency and sophistication, in his later work.

Thus, in *No End (Bez Końca,* 1984), the widow of a lawyer, who at the time of his death was preparing to defend a victim of martial law,

Living with ghosts: Grażyna Szapolowska in *No End*.

gradually becomes involved in the struggle to save the young worker from the authorities; her actions, however, are less the result of growing political commitment than of her being prompted, as it were, by her husband's ghost who, mostly unseen except by the audience, watches over her in her solitude. While the film offers a lucid account of how self-serving bureaucracy and an embattled judiciary make for political and moral compromise ('Martial law was really a defeat for everyone,' Kieślowski told Stok),[6] the director was equally fascinated by the metaphysical and emotional aspects of the story. The film ends with the widow, unable to bear her grief any longer, committing suicide so that she may be reunited with her beloved husband. Politically the film may be despairing, even defeatist, but on a humanistic level, its conclusion, with wife and husband united once more in a world Kieślowski regarded as 'a little better than the one in which we're immersed', is one of transcendent devotion.

It was while preparing *No End* that Kieślowski first embarked on what would become an enduring collaborative partnership with Krzysztof Piesiewicz, a lawyer he met while making a documentary on trials under martial law. (The film was never completed, since Kieślowski found that his camera's presence in the courtrooms seemed to encourage judges to pass unusually lenient sentences, which therefore mitigated against the accuracy of his film!) Because the director felt himself ignorant of court procedure, he invited Piesiewicz to help with the legal details in the script of *No End*; the partnership worked so well that they revived their collaboration for Kieślowski's subsequent *The Decalogue (Dekalog,* 1988), a ten-part series made for Polish television after Piesiewicz suggested the director consider a film about the Ten Commandments and their relevance to the modern world.

Originally, Kieślowski's intention was to write the ten episodes – two of which were shot in alternative longer versions (as *A Short Film About Killing* and *A Short Film About Love*) for cinema release – and then hand them over to ten young, first-time film-makers at the Tor Production House (which Kieślowski was running as deputy to Krzysztof Zanussi). By the time the scripts had reached the first-draft stage, however, Kieślowski liked them so much that he decided to direct them himself (though he did select nine different cameramen for the ten episodes). The result was one of the most impressive achievements in modern film-making. Keeping the political realities of contemporary Polish life in the background, the aim was to focus on the 'internal lives' of the various protagonists – all inhabitants of a Warsaw housing estate – as they made their 'concrete everyday decisions' about various ethical and emotional dilemmas associated in one way or another with the Commandments. Characteristically, Kieślowski refrained from offering simplistic, moralistic comments on what he felt was right or wrong; instead, rather like Eric Rohmer's series of *Contes moraux*, the films were cool, pragmatic studies of the problems faced by people who 'don't really know why they are living';[7] people who feel lonely and uncertain about particular aspects of their lives, and want to achieve some sense of happiness, of belonging, of having done their best with regard to what is 'right' for them. Inevitably, given Kieślowski's self-confessed pessimism, they often fail, or if they succeed, it is usually at a painful price. Besides being a *magnum opus* in its own right, *The Decalogue* is also, as we shall

A Short Film About Killing

see later, of considerable interest for the way in which it anticipates in many respects aspects of the *Three Colours* trilogy: most notably, perhaps, the accent on loneliness and dysfunctional families; the importance of love; and the way in which Kieślowski's narrative forges strange, unexpected connections between different characters.

Kieślowski's next film, again written with Piesiewicz, took him still further away from the specifically Polish experience, not only in that it was his first international co-production, but because its subject matter is perhaps best described as spiritual. *The Double Life of Véronique (La Double vie de Véronique/Podwójne Życie Weroniki,* 1991) concerns the strange, mysterious links between the lives of two physically identical young women born at the same time on the same day: the Polish Weronika, a budding soprano with a weak heart and an indecisive attitude towards her lover, and the French Véronique, who abandons her plans for a musical career after a cardiographic diagnosis, and responds in a determined, positive fashion to an admirer's bizarre methods of courtship. The two never meet (though Weronika sees her double inadvertently taking her photo during a trip to Krakow), but after the Polish girl

Soul sister: Irène Jacob in *The Double Life of Véronique*

collapses and dies during a concert, Véronique not only experiences feelings of inexplicable solitude and sadness, but is somehow forewarned from making the same 'mistakes' that led to her counterpart's death.

Critical reaction to the film was largely enthusiastic, but the critics were a little mystified as to what, precisely, Kieślowski was trying to say: this, emphatically, was his most 'metaphysical' work to date, predicated on a mysterious, almost supernatural connection between its two protagonists. At the same time, however, notwithstanding a visual style described by critic Jonathan Romney, in a review for *Sight and Sound*, as 'luminous, numinous and ominous',[8] Kieślowski firmly grounded his story of 'irrational' presentiments and inexplicable emotions in a recognisable material universe. Quite simply, the film was a brave, unusually successful attempt to evoke and explore the unseen, unfathomable forces – fate and chance – that shape our lives even as we go about our banal everyday business in a tangibly corporeal world.

It was not only in terms of its subject matter, however, that *Véronique* brought Kieślowski closer to the triumph of the *Three Colours* films, but it was also in terms of style. From the relatively simple observational 'realism' of the documentaries and early features, Kieślowski's work had steadily developed into something more complex with regard to narrative and expression. The stories had become far more elliptical, more prone to making mysterious yet resonant connections between characters and objects; visually, the films had become more ornate, using a greater diversity of colours, 'unnatural' lighting, unusual compositions and angles. In short, the films had gradually become more 'poetic', more 'expressionist', culminating in the sophisticated artifice of *Véronique*. It may be that it was this stylistic transformation that gave rise to the occasional accusations against the *Three Colours* films of ambiguity, artiness, even obscurity.

Although *The Double Life of Véronique* was in certain respects Kieślowski's most enigmatic film, it did pave the way for the rather more accessible and, arguably, more assured study of abstract, seemingly inexplicable forces at work in the everyday world that was the *Three Colours* trilogy. Discussing *Véronique*, the director told Danusia Stok:

You make films to give people something, to transport them somewhere else, and it doesn't matter if you transport them to a world of intuition or a world of the intellect. ... A lot of people don't understand the direction in which I'm going. They think ... I've betrayed my way of looking at the world. ... I absolutely don't feel that I've betrayed any of my opinions or my attitude to life. The realm of superstitions, fortune-telling, presentiments, intuition, dreams, all this is the inner life of a human being, and all this is the hardest thing to film. ... I've been trying to get there from the beginning. I'm somebody who doesn't know, somebody who's searching.[9]

With the *Three Colours* trilogy, Kieślowski's search for new, more precise ways to explore people's inner lives would continue, resulting in the most ambitious, challenging films of his career – films that concerned the worlds of intuition *and* of the intellect.

Kieślowski with Jean-Louis Trintignant and Irène Jacob on the set of *Red*

2 Making the Trilogy

As with *The Decalogue*, it was Piesiewicz who suggested the basic thematic idea for the *Three Colours* trilogy of examining how the seminal ideals of the French Revolution – liberty, equality, fraternity – function in the modern world. Again, despite naming and structuring the trilogy after the colours of the French flag, the director decided that the three abstract concepts should be examined not in terms of their political, social or philosophical import, but on an intimate, personal level. Indeed, he claimed:

The idea of the three ideals is just a pretext; it's not especially relevant to today. Any period has its difficulties, and every generation says things were better in the good old days; it's what we tell the younger generation. So our time is as good as any other to make these films....

What interested me and Piesiewicz was to look at freedom from a personal aspect, which is more universal. If you were to speak to, say, Bosnians or Croatians about their idea of political freedom, they'd contradict each other, whereas they'd probably have the same idea of personal freedom, or of love. There are so many things that separate people around the world today that one ought perhaps to look for factors that unite people ... just to state that such things exist.

Having won wide international acclaim for *The Decalogue* and *The Double Life of Véronique*, Kieślowski had little difficulty finding backing for such an ambitious project. In the event, he declared himself very satisfied with the work of both Yvon Crenn, the executive producer who oversaw the films' budget on a daily basis, and Marin Karmitz, the Romanian-born radical director-turned-distributor, exhibitor and producer whose French company, MK2, had already made films by the likes of the Taviani Brothers, Godard, Chabrol and Malle. It was not, however, the fact that the trilogy was a French–Polish–Swiss co-production that brought about the decision to set each film in a different country:

Of course money had something to do with it, but that came at a later stage. It was the ideas that counted: if we were to make films about these three words, we felt we should broaden the trilogy beyond France, because they're not just French ideals. Most of our money was French, so that made one choice obvious; making one film in Poland was a natural decision for me; for the third, it took a while to decide. We thought of Italy and England, but then we decided to make it a French-speaking country, and chose Switzerland. Of course, we could have changed the three countries around, but then the scripts and characters would have been different. Environment is not the most important thing, but it does help describe character – people use different languages and have slightly different things in mind when they use certain words.

The scripts, which went through four drafts before being translated from Polish for the final versions, were produced by Kieślowski and Piesiewicz's usual method: the latter came up with 'general ideas', while the director himself wrote the various drafts, making changes at every stage after discussions with his partner, before further comment was invited from 'screenplay consultants' Agnieszka Holland, Edward Zebrowski and Edward Klosinski, film-maker friends from Poland who had served (unofficially) in this capacity for many years. (It is illuminating to compare the fourth-draft screenplays, as published by Faber and Faber, with the finished films: although Kieślowski excised and condensed many scenes – and changed a few details – during shooting, nothing of significance was lost. Indeed, however promising the screenplays, the films themselves are noticeably richer.)

In selecting his actors and technicians, Kieślowski was able to call on the services of many of the finest talents in the French and Polish film industries. After their successful collaboration on *The Double Life of Véronique*, the director was keen to work again with Irène Jacob, and wrote *Red* with the actress in mind: 'To play someone like Valentine – very delicate, sensitive, very good – you have to have it within yourself; it can be acted, but only to a certain degree. Since I knew Irène was like that, I had the courage to write the script.' The choice of cinematographers also was crucial. As with *The Decalogue*, Kieślowski decided on different cameramen for each film: for *Blue*, he chose Slawomir Idziak, who had shot two of Kieślowski's early films (the 1973 TV drama *Pedestrian Subway* and the 1976 feature *The Scar*) as well as *Decalogue 5* (*A Short Film About Killing*) and *The Double Life of Véronique*; he felt Idziak would be especially adept at conveying the protagonist's subjective state of mind; for *White*, he chose Edward Klosinski, who had shot *Decalogue 2*; and for *Red*, Piotr Sobocinski, who had worked on the third and ninth parts of the series. For a work in which colours would be used not as mere decoration but to carry meaning, working with able, imaginative cameramen was clearly of the utmost importance.

Another major creative talent from Kieślowski's earlier work was the composer Zbigniew Preisner, whose haunting scores had graced *No End*, *The Decalogue* and been memorably integrated into the narrative of *The Double Life of Véronique*. Music would contribute directly to the story of *Blue*, and play a significant role in enhancing all three of the trilogy's films' moods and meanings since the overall structure of the

The Scar, shot by Slawomir Idziak, cinematographer for *Blue*

trilogy itself would be, in terms of rhythm, tone and range, not so very unlike that of a symphony.

Amazingly, given its complexity, the trilogy was made quickly; according to Kieślowski, making the whole thing, from conception to completion, took about two-and-a-half years. Actual shooting took about nine weeks for each film, with breaks between filming kept to a minimum; indeed, the day after filming for *Blue* was completed, Kieślowski began shooting the Parisian scenes for *White*. The production process was speeded up even further by Kieślowski's habit of shooting one film at the same time as he was editing its predecessor. In this way, he was able to achieve the remarkable feat of premièring the three films at major festivals within a few months of each other: *Blue* in September 1993 at Venice, *White* in February 1994 at Berlin and, finally, *Red* in May 1994 at Cannes.

3 *Three Colours: Blue*

That *Blue* is about personal rather than political notions of freedom is at once apparent from the social and economic status of the protagonist: Julie (Juliette Binoche), the widow of a renowned French composer, is well to do, has no evident financial problems, and no apparent political affiliations. Her struggle to find freedom takes place not in the political arena but in the realm of the emotions, as she strives to achieve a sense of self-suffiency, stability and independence following the death, in a car crash, of her husband Patrice and daughter Anna.

In what is essentially a prologue to the story proper, we see that Julie's predicament is, typically for Kieślowski, the result of chance. The film opens with a sequence of shots showing the family's Alfa Romeo speeding along an autoroute through the blue night: we see Anna's hand holding a blue piece of paper in the wind; Anna's face staring through the rear window, followed by traffic and tunnel lights from her point of view, distorted into streaks of colour (including, at one point, lines of red, white and blue); then, in a stationary shot, from beneath the car, of the girl returning (out of focus) from having taken a pee at the roadside, fluid dripping ominously from the brake cable. Cut to a country road and a teenage hitchhiker failing repeatedly to balance a ball on the end of a stick: only after the Alfa Romeo emerges out of the blue morning mist to speed past him does he get lucky in his game (mirroring his good fortune in not being given a lift), but his triumphant smile is immediately wiped from his face by the sound of the car crashing into a tree.

Already, the muted expressionism of Kieślowski's very precise use of sound and image is apparent from his deployment of colour, composition, cutting and unexpected, off-screen noise. Throughout the film, blue will be used not as a symbol of 'freedom', but to create moods of melancholy and coldness, and to draw attention to the resonant emotional associations conjured up by objects and places in Julie's mind. Likewise, Anna's distorted view of the speeding traffic anticipates Kieślowski's use of extreme close-ups, very shallow focus, and wide-angle shots to home in on his protagonist's mental state. Without resorting to

26 | BFI MODERN CLASSICS

Muted expressionism: the opening sequence of *Blue*

the near-continuous use of explicit dialogue or voice-over narration generally favoured by even the most sophisticated contemporary American cinema for the exploration of inner emotions (e.g. the films of Woody Allen, Terrence Malick, John Sayles or Martin Scorsese), or even to the clumsy, contrived 'subjective camera' style of the cautiously experimental *Lady in the Lake* (Robert Montgomery, 1947), Kieślowski focuses so closely and precisely on Julie, and positions her so carefully within the frame, that we are continually aware, without her needing to verbalise her feelings, of her intensely private responses to the world around her.

Thus, as the story of Julie's attempts to come to terms with her loss of husband and child begins, we see, through her blurred vision, a doctor approaching her hospital bed; as he tells her of her husband's death, Kieślowski cuts to a remarkably tight close-up of her eye with the doctor reflected in the pupil, so that we both receive essential narrative information *and* witness Julie's reaction from unnaturally close quarters. After she sobs silently at the news that Anna is also dead, the melancholy mood is suddenly broken by the sight and sound of shattering glass (the second of many 'heightened' loud noises in the film), as Julie, angry at what has befallen her, creates a distraction for the night nurse by

Reflections in a grieving eye: Julie's reaction to the doctor

smashing a window, and raids the drugs cabinet for a suicidal overdose. Her will to survive is too strong, however; she cannot swallow the pills.

Henceforth, after watching the funeral service on a miniature television brought her by family friend Olivier (Benoît Régent), Julie sets about reconstructing her life through an extreme form of self-denial; to ensure that it is free from pain, she decides to rid herself, steadily and surely, of material goods, memories, relationships and responsibilities associated with her past. Even before she leaves the hospital, however, she receives an 'omen' that fate may have decreed otherwise: not only does a journalist track her down, enquiring in vain whether it's true that Julie was really the writer of Patrice's music, but at the very moment of the journalist's arrival, Julie is also visited, as it were, by a funereal fragment of a concerto he (she?) was composing to commemorate the Unification of Europe.[10] 'Visited', in that the crashing chords seem to come out of nowhere: Kieślowski suggests the music's almost supernatural provenance by showing Julie first dozing in a chair with an unexplained blue light playing over her face, then, having been woken by the music, looking startled and mystified towards the camera (which not only draws back from her and then returns, but bathes the scene in a blue wash), as if the music itself were a (blue?) physical presence. As the blue wash evaporates, we hear the journalist's voice say 'Bonjour', and the screen briefly fades to black – with the music continuing – before

Kind of blue: Julie receives a musical visitation

returning to 'normal'. The effect of this scene is multiple: to establish Julie's desire for privacy, to show the impossibility of escaping the past – people, objects, memories will always intrude – and to suggest not only that she may well have written (or at the very least collaborated in) her husband's music but that artistic creation can be literally inspired, even involuntary. (Kieślowski himself described the creative process as partly a matter of 'stealing' ideas – 'afterwards I can't even remember where I stole them from'[11] – or of 'drawing things in' that already exist somewhere out in the universe.)

These short, virtually wordless early scenes establish the style (and, indeed, content) for much of what follows in the film. Julie will sporadically be 'visited' by brief musical fragments, accompanied visually by blue flashes, washes and/or fade-outs for which, physically, there is no explanation; music and colour alike serve partly to denote the abstract forces that stand as obstacles to her quest for personal freedom. When she returns to the family farmhouse, she determines at once to sell it and dispose of most of her possessions (including, found in her handbag, one of Anna's blue lollipops wrapped in the same blue paper we saw fluttering in the wind at the start of the film), taking only a few basic belongings – most notably a blue chandelier from the 'blue room' – to the flat she rents in order to start a new, isolated, anonymous life in Paris.

It is not only music and material goods, however, that Julie seeks to avoid, but people. Before moving to Paris, she elicits a confession from Olivier of long-standing love; she invites him to her home and, on the bare mattress which is the only remaining piece of furniture in the house, perfunctorily has sex with him. For her, there is no passion; this is a cool, determined attempt to kill his love for her. The next morning, she wakes him with a smile and a cup of coffee, tells him he should now be able to see that she is as imperfect as other women (and therefore won't miss her), and leaves before he can dress, deliberately grazing her hand along a stone wall as she goes, as if to prepare herself for the pain her self-denial and solitude will bring her.

In Paris she plans to live without company, pleasure, or responsibilities (though she does make financial provision for her mother and household staff); it is as if she wants her solitude, her 'freedom', to serve as a wall between herself and the chaos and sadness of the outside world. Chance, however, allows no such thing. The first intrusion upon her privacy comes when a man fleeing muggers in the street thunders up the stairs to her flat and beats her door in search of sanctuary; terrified, she stands immobile, listening to his attackers drag him away, before emerging on to the landing, dressed only in a T-shirt, to check that they've gone. As luck would have it, the wind bangs her door closed behind her; locked out for the night, she is not only 'visited' once more by the music, but she makes eye contact with Lucille (Charlotte Véry), who lives downstairs – a stripper who later determines to become Julie's grateful friend, after Julie, reluctant as ever to get involved, refuses to sign a neighbours' petition demanding that Lucille leave the building.

Other factors invade and disturb her solitary existence, but only momentarily; so caught up in her own world is she that, sitting in a park, she doesn't even notice an old woman struggling to deposit a bottle in a recycling bin. Olivier tracks her down to a café, after his cleaner accidentally spots her in the crowded Rue Mouffetard where she lives, but she sends him away; a nest of mice (a grotesque echo of the family life Julie has lost) settles in her closet until she sets a neighbour's cat upon them; she is haunted by a local busker's flute melody, oddly reminiscent of the music that erupts repeatedly in her head, until she asks him where

Julie alone in her new flat

he heard the tune ('I invent lots of things'); and Antoine, the boy who witnessed the crash, traces her through her doctor and returns her crucifix (found near the car) which Julie, after saying that 'nothing is important', tells him, unsentimentally and without waiting for thanks, to keep.[12] The only real human contact initiated by Julie is with her mother (Emmanuelle Riva), whom she visits in a nursing home. Ironically, however, as Julie tries to explain that her former happy life is over and that she no longer wants the 'traps' of possessions, friends, memories and love, her mother is unable properly to understand; she too is preoccupied by a past that she cannot, or will not, let go of (she keeps speaking to Julie as if she were her own dead sister, and surrounds herself with old family photos), and notices little but the strange, lonely images of men performing daredevil aerial feats that play constantly on her television.[13]

Nothing can break down the barriers Julie has erected to ensure her solitary freedom until Lucille decides, out of the blue, to ask for help. Summoned late one night to the strip club in the Pigalle where

Privacy invaded: Julie with Lucille

Julie's image on television

Lucille works, Julie finds the girl upset after spotting her father in the audience; though Julie does nothing except turn up, put her hand on Lucille's shoulder and listen to her story, the girl thanks her for simply being there.[14] It is, ironically, during this meeting at the strip club that Lucille inadvertently sets Julie on her path to redemption or, at least, back to a more 'normal' life allowing for full human interaction. On a television screen, Lucille suddenly points out Julie's face, in a photo taken by the journalist at the hospital: the programme is a documentary about Patrice, in which Olivier reveals that the European Council has asked him to complete the unfinished Concerto (Julie wrongly believed she had destroyed the only copy of the score), and in which snapshots are shown of Patrice both with his wife and, to Julie's bewilderment, with another, unfamiliar woman dressed in blue. The next day she visits Olivier, who admits that he decided to finish the Concerto to provoke Julie into action, into showing some sort of emotion. She tells him he has no right to work on the music, and asks about the woman in the photo; he, in turn, is surprised to learn she had no inkling of Patrice's long-standing affair with the woman, a lawyer. (Are we, then, perhaps to infer that Julie was at a remove from reality, and too complacently caught up in her family life, even before the car crash? Although Kieślowski gives no proper evidence with which we might construct any firm impression of her earlier life or character, it is, I think, a distinct possibility, given her paradoxical attempts, during the film's timespan, to idealise and 'fix' her past by refusing properly to come to terms with it.)

Immediately, Julie searches out her husband's mistress, Sandrine (Florence Pernel), at the law courts, and eventually confronts her in the toilets of a restaurant, only to see that she is pregnant. Calmly, Sandrine confesses that the father is Patrice (who died before learning of the pregnancy), and that he loved her – which, noticing around Sandrine's neck a crucifix identical to her own, Julie has already divined. Leaving quickly without confirming whether, as Sandrine expects, she will hate her, Julie goes to a (blue, again signifying melancholy and solitude) swimming pool where, in the past, she has indulged her desire for privacy; diving in, she stays under the water long enough to suggest she

The will to live: Julie emerges from the depths of despair

may once more be considering suicide. However, again her survival instinct is too strong, and she bursts to the surface, spitting water and gasping for breath.

The film's final scenes chart Julie's steady progress towards reintegration into a world of unrepressed emotions, where she can be true to her needs and her grief (hitherto she has wept only at the hospital). She goes to see her mother but, recognising the futility of trying to explain her situation, leaves without a word. She visits Olivier, and (with music blasting forth as her finger traces, in extreme close-up and shallow focus, the blue notes on the manuscript) helps him to complete the Concerto's final chorus, an hommage to Patrice's beloved Van den Budenmayer. She then returns to the farmhouse (which she has now instructed her *notaire* not to sell), where she welcomes Sandrine, telling her that she would like the baby to have both Patrice's name (as Sandrine already intended) and his house. Julie, it seems, has accepted the destiny her will tried so hard to deny: Sandrine reveals that Patrice

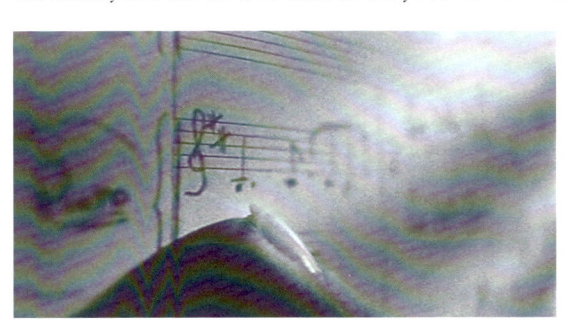

A note of optimism as she rediscovers the creative urge

34 | BFI MODERN CLASSICS

THE 'THREE COLOURS' TRILOGY | 35

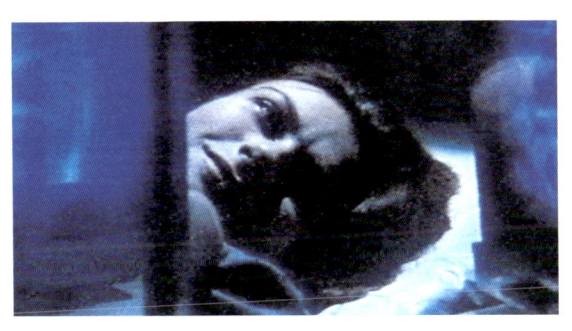

Touched by love: Julie, Antoine, Julie's mother and Sandrine, brought together in Kieślowski's 'magnificent coda'

often told her not only that his wife was good, generous and dependable, but that she wanted to be.

Julie returns to her flat to finish the orchestration of the chorus; upon its completion she calls Olivier, who says he will not have anything to do with the music unless it is made known that it is now theirs, and not Patrice's alone. At last, Julie agrees to admit the part she has played in its creation. Moreover, having finally realised that her feelings for her husband were based on a lie, she feels free to accept the love of Olivier (who has bought and kept the mattress they once slept on);[15] in a reversal of what occurred before, she goes to him, leaving the flat she had tried to turn into a fortress ... or prison.

After she walks out the door (shot, as often before, through the blue chandelier), the film's magnificent coda begins, a non-narrative montage that shows, in turn, all the major characters while simultaneously allowing us to hear, in full for the first time, the eight-minute chorus. With the camera drifting dreamily from one image to the next, as if each of the characters were somehow linked in a continuum of time and space, we see: Julie and Olivier making love; Antoine waking in bed, fingering the crucifix around his neck; Julie's mother falling asleep (or, perhaps, dying?) as a nurse comes to check on her; Lucille pensive in the Pigalle sex-club; a (blue) ultrasound-scan of the unborn child, watched by Sandrine; and finally, as at the beginning, Julie's eye in extreme close-up, before we see her face at a window – silent, slightly tearful and, as the image fades with a reflection of blue sky rising slowly across her features, giving a small, tentative smile.

That this sequence, resonant with associations of waking and sleeping, birth and death, solitude and sexual communion, is more than just a neat way of tying up the story's various threads is clear from the words Kieślowski chose to be sung for the final chorus:

Though I speak with the tongue of angels, if I have not love, I am become as hollow brass. Though I have the gift of prophecy, and understand all mysteries and all knowledge, and though I have enough faith to move the mightiest mountains, if I have not love, I am nothing.

Love is patient, love is kind. It bears all things, it hopes all things. Love never fails. For prophecies shall fail, tongues shall cease, knowledge will wither away. And now shall abide faith, hope and love; but the greatest of these is love.

This text, adapted from St Paul's First Letter to the Corinthians (13: 1–13), not only highlights the supremacy of love over other considerations, but it also throws light on the meaning of the final montage and the entire film. Unintentionally and unwittingly, Julie has by her generosity and dependability, and by her fundamental *goodness*, touched each of the characters shown in the montage: their lives have somehow been marked, even enhanced by their encounters with her,

Free to grieve: Julie's tentative smile

united in a common humanity by her love, just as they are brought together by Kieślowski's camera and cutting.[16] Love never fails; it may be painful, even (as we shall see in *White*) cruel, but it dominates our lives, and we ignore it at our peril. Human interaction is, in the end, inevitable.

Personal freedom, then, is shown not only to be impossible, but to be something which, in Kieślowski's words, 'people don't really want': he felt able to celebrate Julie's final acceptance that she needs other people, her abandoning of her quest for complete independence, because, he said, 'Love is a much more human emotion than the desire for freedom'. At the same time, however, it can be argued that, in recognising her needs and, consequently, the humanity she shares with others, Julie does finally achieve a freedom of sorts. Though her future may be uncertain – the final image shows her behind glass, suggesting perhaps that she is still, as it were, at a remove from reality, and has yet to travel further before she achieves a full emotional recovery – she has been freed from both the imprisoning illusions she entertained about her marriage, and the falsehoods that she encouraged regarding her contributions to her husband's work. Consequently, she feels free at last to grieve, to accept both the love of others and the effect she has upon others, and to face her destiny – to acknowledge that she, too, is human, and wants to live.

Shot, scored, scripted and performed with great sensitivity (Juliette Binoche's customary restraint and mask-like face are especially well used by Kieślowski to suggest Julie's self-willed impassivity), *Blue* is an admirably tough, penetrating study of loss, grief and loneliness; even the deeply affirmative tone of its coda is free of maudlin sentimentality. As the first episode in what promised to be an extraordinarily affecting triptych, it served its purpose beautifully. The only question, for many, must have been how Kieślowski could possibly keep up the dramatic momentum.

4 *Three Colours: White*

Cinemagoers accustomed to the generally serious tone of Kieślowski's work, and expecting the second film of the *Three Colours* trilogy to be in the same dramatic register as *Blue*, may have been surprised to discover that *White* was a droll black comedy, complete with such generic staples as missing corpses, cunning schemes and sexual humiliation. Perhaps also unexpected would have been the fact that Kieślowski's exploration of 'equality' was, yet again, not primarily political; though the film derives much humour from its sardonic depiction of the dog-eat-dog mores of contemporary, capitalist Poland, social comment is included first and foremost as a contextualising reflection of the emotional conflict between its two protagonists.

While the film's visual style (in terms of lighting, camera-movement, colour-filters, etc.) is admittedly less ornate, less expressionist and generally more conventionally naturalistic than that of its predecessor, from the opening scenes there can be no doubt as to the precision of Kieślowski's *mise en scène*. The first sequence cuts between shots of a large suitcase on an airport conveyor belt, and a man's feet walking along a city pavement. Although we have no idea of how the

A case of destiny and premonition: the opening sequence of *White*

images relate to one another, the way Kieślowski's camera lingers on the case, investing it with some as yet unknown significance, indicates that there is indeed an important link between luggage and man. (In fact, as we shall discover, the shots of the case, a flash-forward in time, introduce at once the motifs of destiny – recalling *Blue* – and prescience.) Then, as the camera rises to reveal the man as Karol (Zbigniew Zamachowski), it's clear that he is anxious: as he dashes along to the law courts, the first other people we see – a young couple kissing in the street and a gendarme – serve respectively to anticipate Karol's problems with sexual passion and with the law. The streak of pigeon droppings (the first flash of white) that fall on Karol's suit as he stands on the court steps introduces the theme of humiliation – sexual, economic, social and physical – which will weave throughout the film.

The reason for this Polish hairdresser's presence in a Paris courtroom soon becomes apparent: his French wife Dominique (Julie Delpy) is filing for divorce on the grounds that their marriage is unconsummated. Complaining of the inequality he faces in court due to his inability to speak fluent French, Karol attempts to explain his problem: when they first met and were together in Poland, he experienced no difficulty satisfying Dominique, but after moving to France and marrying

'The first flash of white', and the first whiff of humiliation for Karol

her, he just couldn't sustain his physical passion – life and work abroad, for this exile, are apparently too stressful. Recovery is merely a matter of time, he claims, since love remains – at which point Kieślowski includes an overlit flashback, from Karol's point of view, of Dominique, seen from behind in white veil and wedding dress, walking out of a gloomy church into the bright sunlight, and turning around to smile. The dreamlike tone of this shot (later repeated), at once subtly ironic and unashamedly romantic, implies that the hapless Pole may be living in a fantasy world, which, indeed, he is, as becomes plain when Dominique insists that she no longer loves him in a public disavowal that sends Karol off to vomit, privately, into a (white) toilet bowl. Already, we can see that Kieślowski is taking a different perspective of love than in *Blue*; here, not only is love more comic, but we can see that it may be painful and cruel, or that love may even be just a figment of the romantic imagination.

The humiliations continue as Karol (suffering involuntarily what Julie in *Blue* chooses to do) is systematically stripped of his possessions, identity and confidence. After Dominique drives off, dumping his suitcase ('That's all') outside the court, he loses his bank card in a cash-machine; when he enters the bank, only to learn that the account has been frozen by Dominique, the teller cuts the card with scissors before his very eyes. Karol's wincing expression clearly points to the act's castratory connotations. (Small wonder that later, shivering in the cold night air, he is so absorbed in self-pity that, on seeing an old man struggling to deposit a bottle in a recycling bin, he simply smiles, ruefully, without thinking to offer help.) Then, after discovering the keys to his and Dominique's hairdressing salon, where she finds him asleep in the morning, he fails once more in his attempts to make love. Not only does she angrily promise that she'll win every battle they wage, and accuse him of understanding nothing of her love, need or hatred for him, but she sets alight the salon's white curtains, explaining that she'll tell the police that he torched the place out of a desire (and here she shows unwitting foresight) for revenge. In panic, Karol makes his escape.

Notwithstanding such setbacks, the impoverished, homeless exile can't entirely abandon his fantasies: passing a shop, he gazes wistfully at a pale plaster bust of a woman (apparently, it reminds him of his wife), before heading for a Metro station where he begs for money by 'playing' sentimental old Polish tunes on a paper and comb. By the time a sympathetic (if equally morose) compatriot, Mikolaj (Janusz Gajos), stops to talk, share a bottle and offer to take him back to Poland, Karol has lost his passport and is virtually penniless, so that Mikolaj is moved

Cold fire: Dominique anticipates Karol's desire for revenge

to suggest a strange deal: if Karol will kill a man, who is suicidal but won't take his own life lest it further upset his loving wife and children, Karol will be paid enough money to return to Poland and survive for six months. Karol, however, turns the offer down, for he still loves Dominique and wants to be reunited with her.

Hoping to demonstrate her beauty to Mikolaj, he takes him to her apartment, next to which – fittingly, given the title and subject matter of Godard's film – is a billboard poster of Brigitte Bardot in *Le Mépris (Contempt)*. 'Beautiful – but isn't she a bit over the hill?' jokes Mikolaj, deliberately getting hold of the wrong end of the stick. As they stand in the darkness looking up at her window, they see Dominique silhouetted behind her curtains, embracing another man. Distraught, Karol rushes

back into the Metro to phone her, thus engineering for himself the ultimate humiliation: she makes him listen, entranced but horrified, to her loud moans as she has sex with her visitor. To add insult to injury, all he has left after the phone call is a two-franc coin. Defeated, he agrees to accompany Mikolaj back to Poland, but on his own terms: throwing away his hairdressing diplomas, proud symbols of his past triumphs, he punches air-holes in his suitcase and persuades Mikolaj to transport him home as baggage. Destiny is at work.

A cuckold's-view: Karol's ultimate humiliation as Dominique makes love with another man

Again we see the suitcase being propelled inexorably forth on the conveyor belt and, this time, being ferried precariously on its bumpy ride to the plane; now, however, we are aware of its contents, and therefore more deeply concerned as to its future. Not everyone is so sympathetic to the luggage's safety: Karol's reacquaintance with his homeland first takes the form of being stolen by airport baggage-handlers, who unsuspectingly drive their booty into the snowy countryside and, on breaking open the case to find a man with only a Russian watch, a two-franc piece and a pair of scissors to his name, beat him up before dumping him in a rubbish tip. 'Home at last!' he sighs, surveying a flock of white gulls scavenging among the garbage, before grabbing the now shattered plaster bust he stole before leaving Paris.

All is not lost, however, for Karol has a brother, Jurek (Jerzy Stuhr), who kindly takes him in to recuperate – but on condition he help out a little with the work in his hairdressing salon. (In *White* every relationship, however close, is at least partly predicated on some sort of economic exchange, involving love as currency.) Immediately, Karol sets about repairing both the bust and his dreams; now, instead of the bright memories of Dominique at their wedding, he harbours fantasies (premonitions?) of her walking, sad and dressed in black, into an empty, darkened room. (Intriguingly, the first such fantasies occur immediately after he has tried in vain to toss the despised two-franc coin into a river;

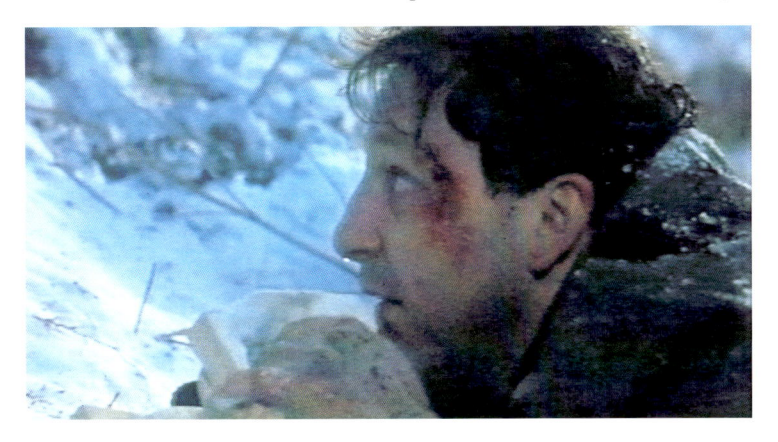

'Home at last!': Karol down and out in Poland

the fact that it sticks to his palm seems to steel his mettle.) First, however, he must find his feet again, which means that he must play by the rules of the new Poland, a place of corruption, violence, greed and dishonesty.

Evidently, Karol still hopes to win back Dominique. Between kissing the bust and learning French from audiotapes (including the past subjunctive: 'Would that I had pleased', indeed!), Karol sets about finding himself a job. A client at the salon tells him of a money-changing joint, where he manages to persuade the shady boss that he needs a security guard. He's not very impressive as a hard man, and looks distinctly uncomfortable with the tear-gas gun he's given, but he's keen and, besides, appears stupid enough for his boss openly to discuss his dubious schemes with his partner without bothering to check if Karol is listening. Happily for Karol, they underestimate his determination to prove himself: after eavesdropping on their plans to buy up some farmland which big companies like Ikea intend to develop for warehouses, Karol exchanges his earnings for dollars, buys a litre of expensive vodka, and visits a tight-fisted old farmer who, the bottle drained, agrees to sell his tiny plot – right in the middle of the area to be developed – for five thousand dollars. Karol's fortunes are on the mend.

Still, needs must if he is to hit the big time, and after stealing a page from the directory in a broken telephone booth, Karol traces Mikolaj to ask if the offer of killing his suicidal friend still stands. It does, but when Karol goes to honour his underworld-style assignation in the city subway, he finds that the would-be victim is Mikolaj. (Kieślowski's use of the subway seems to symbolise the depths of despair.) After asking 'Are you sure?', Karol takes out a gun – in the new Poland, he observes, 'You can buy anything' – and shoots; his friend and saviour staggers, then opens his eyes. It was a blank (had Karol foreseen Mikolaj's intentions?), though the next shot, he tearfully promises, will be for real. No longer keen to die, Mikolaj insists that Karol take his payment anyway, which is accepted as a loan, before they go out together drinking on the bright sunlit ice, where they joyfully agree that 'Everything is possible'.

Or so it seems, if you have sufficient will, cunning and cash in a society where everything's for sale. Karol is not a bad guy; he's just pragmatic in his determination to win back his wife, and will even reinvent himself according to the rules of the game the world around him is playing. By the time the boss he has 'cheated' catches up with him, strong-arm tactics are of no avail. Karol has made an airtight will so that, should he die, everything he owns will pass to the Church, and he sells the plots he has bought at a 1,000 per cent profit. With Mikolaj as his partner, he sets up a company, buying and selling black-market goods with such energy and success that he soon has a Volvo, designer suits, and is having a house built. Where once he was down and out in Paris, Warsaw is now at his feet. But while he has become a new man, the past still hangs heavy; he still dreams of Dominique who, as impassive as the bust that looks down on his bed, won't answer his calls.

If fortunes can be reversed, so may plans. Whereas Mikolaj wanted someone to kill him so that his (real) suicidal tendencies wouldn't upset his wife, Karol could kill himself off – or at least fake his death – to arouse not only his wife's greed but her guilt and remorse. After changing his will so that all he owns is left to her, replacing his passport with a fake, and acquiring a body to bury (Karol's chauffeur purchases 'a Russian import', unrecognisable after its previous owner leaned too far out of a train window), Karol drops his two-franc piece – souvenir of past poverty and humiliation – into the coffin, before disappearing to observe his own funeral from a safe, discreet distance.

Everything for sale: Karol inspects a new 'Russian import'
(Overleaf) 'Everything is possible'

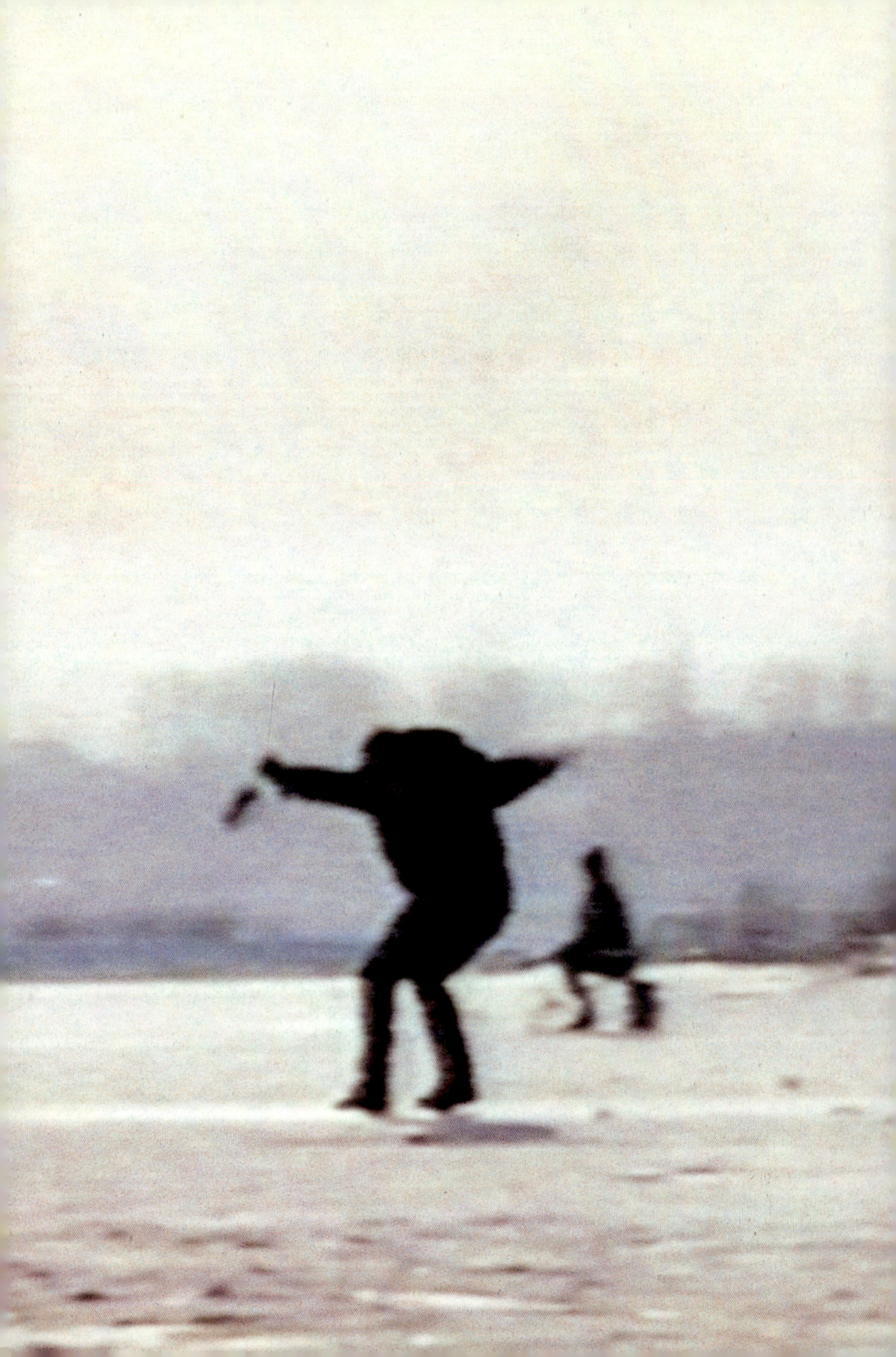

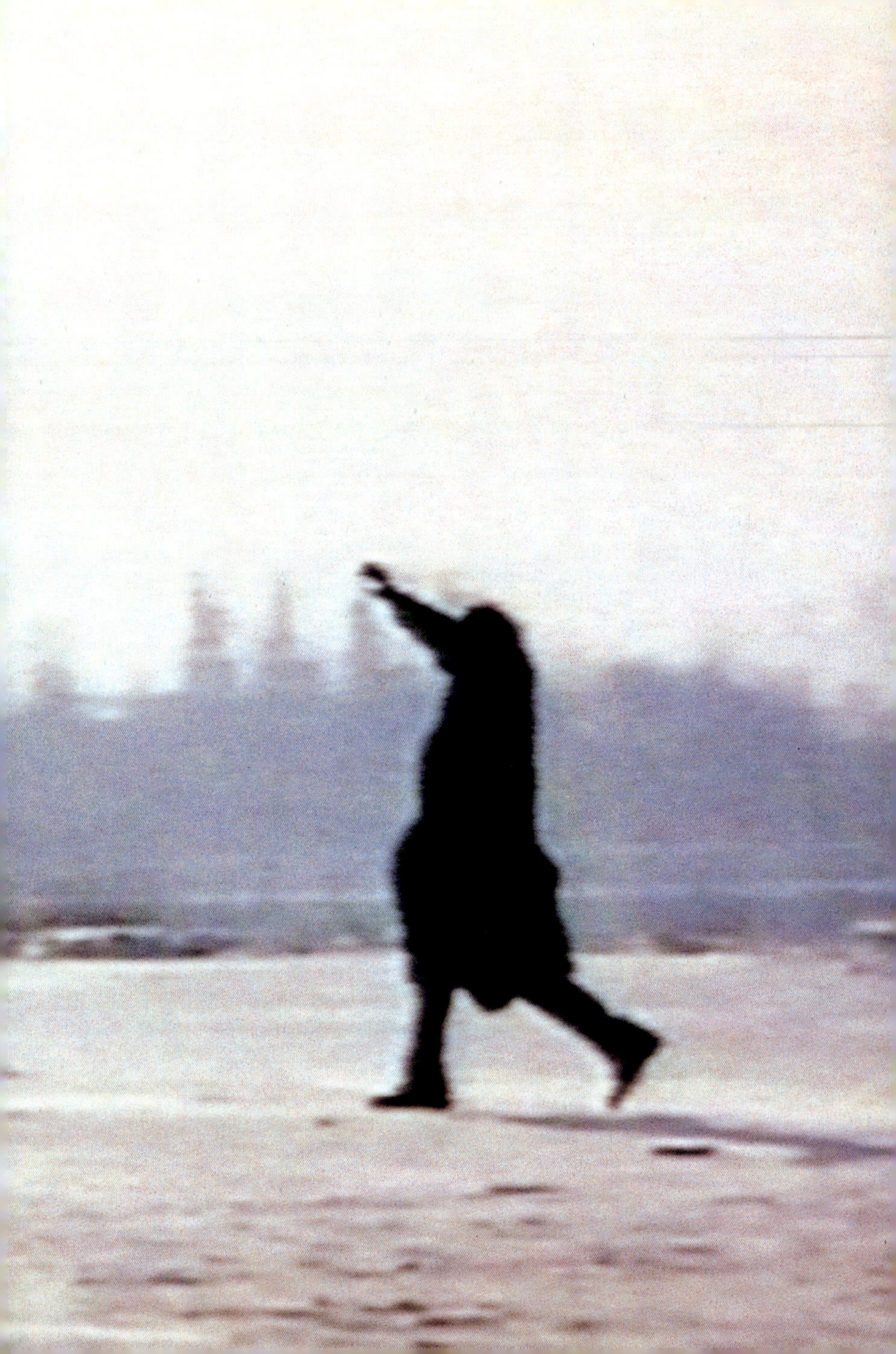

As planned Dominique attends, sufficiently tearful for Karol, between smiles of satisfaction, to feel a pang of pity. Revenge must run its course, however, and after the ceremony, she enters her hotel room, sad and alone as in Karol's fantasies, only to find him naked in bed, waiting for her. Bewildered but reassured by his caress that he is not a ghost, she allows him to kiss her; after the screen fades briefly to black, we see them making love, at which point it fades to black again, their moans continuing until the moment of her orgasm, when she screams and the blank screen turns a blinding white. Fade in again on their two heads on the pillow: 'You moaned even louder than on the phone,' says Karol, highlighting Kieślowski's thesis, already clear from his depiction of

contemporary Poland, that people don't want equality, they just want to be more 'equal' (i.e. better, stronger, richer and more privileged) than others.

As if to emphasise the point, Karol is not content merely to have tricked his wife into returning to him in Poland; now, even though their love, consummated, has put them on an equal footing, he must gain the upper hand, make her suffer as she made him. After gazing fondly at her sleeping form and rearranging her hair (old habits die hard!), he leaves in silence, knowing the police will soon arrive, according to plan, to suggest

'Equality' regained in post-coital bliss

she colluded in his death in order to benefit from the will. Unsurprisingly, her protestations that her husband – whom she now again loves – is really alive carry no weight; too late, she sees she is trapped.

As observed above, however, Karol is not a bad man; he simply wants to make her understand the potency of his need, his love and, perhaps, his hatred, as she once expected him to understand hers. Back in hiding with his brother, therefore, he arranges for her defence by an expensive lawyer who expects, in time, to secure her freedom. Meanwhile, Karol sneaks out to the prison and, looking up at her window (as he once did to see her embrace another man), he watches her signal to him, with her hands, that when her liberty is restored, she would like to marry him again. With tears in his eyes, as the image fades to black, he smiles.

Though often very funny, the content of *White* is such that the film's meaning is entirely in keeping with that of *Blue*. Several themes reappear: the need to let go of the past, while at the same time acknowledging its existence, in order to proceed with the present; the sense of life as an arena in which fate, freedom of will and pure chance are in continual interplay; the way lives may be haunted by feelings about those who are absent or dead; the way inanimate objects and places may

Imprisoned by love: Dominique proposes a fresh start

be invested with an emotional resonance derived from the part they play in our past or future; and the sense that love, in all its many, often perverse manifestations, is the prime motivator behind human action. Here, at least until the end, love is not the healing force it was in *Blue*; it is depicted as something that can be a more selfish, possessive passion, which embraces manipulation, cruelty and vengefulness. And yet, if allowed to mature, it can grow into something more mutually beneficial. Only at the film's end do Karol and Dominique come to recognise their real and sustaining love for each other. At the start, they were still too prone, respectively, to romantic fantasy and selfish petulance to realise that genuine love requires time and mutual understanding in order to develop. And during the year or so that constitutes *White*'s timespan, they come to see that the cruelties they inflict on each other are in fact declarations of love and that deep down, they do need one another.

Stylistically, too, the film is a fitting follow-up to *Blue*, with Kieślowski's economic, carefully detailed direction once more investing the elliptical narrative with a wealth of meaning. The colour of the title is this time used to primarily ironic effect, highlighting banal phenomena with strong metaphorical resonances (the wintry Polish landscape, the scavenging gulls, toilet bowl and pigeon droppings), or Karol's misguided fantasies (the wedding ceremony, the plaster bust); even the fade to white that marks Dominique's orgasm (which also constitutes the climax of Karol's own sexual recovery) coincides with the fruition of his vengeful plan. At the same time, just as *White* proffers an account of love as an emotion which may be either blind, cruel, possessive and immature, or warm, curative, transforming and mutually advantageous, so the colour white has a double-edged resonance in the film, evocative of purity and filth, both physical and moral.

Likewise, Preisner's score makes fine use of a lively, tango-like tune and a fulsomely romantic piano motif to underline the film's comic moments, while at the same time alerting us to the more serious undertones by means of a plaintive, lonely-sounding melody for oboe or clarinet, just as the acting (more extrovert than in *Blue*, but unusually understated in comparison to the performances in most comedies) achieves throughout a careful balance between meticulous comic timing and emotional veracity. *White* is a deft black comedy with genuine thematic substance; not only does it succeed in its own right, but it provides a welcome and probably quite necessary drop in emotional intensity between the more draining first and third stories; it is the lull before the final storm. Again, if one views the trilogy in symphonic terms, its often jaunty mood and fast-paced narrative suggest that it may be seen as a delightful *scherzo allegretto*, wisely sandwiched between the sombre *moderato* of *Blue* and the magisterially expansive *allegro non troppo* of *Red*.

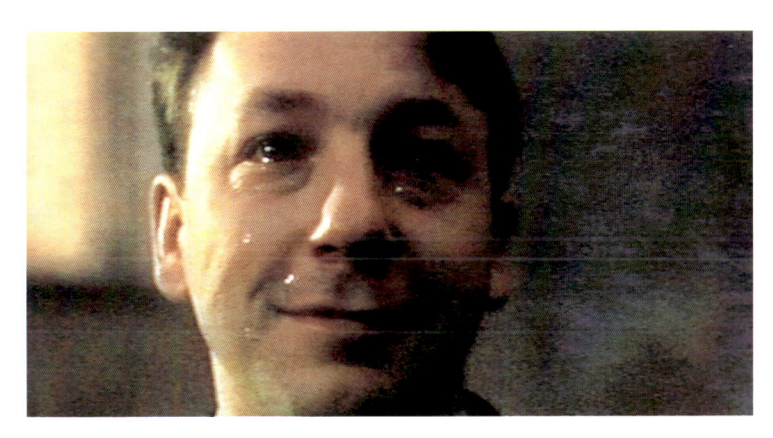

Free to forgive: Karol's tearful smile

5 *Three Colours: Red*

Of the final instalment in his trilogy, Kieślowski said:

> *Red* is my most personal film, I think. It reflects not only my way of thinking about life, but about cinema: that film can come just that little bit closer to literature than one would imagine. It's a bit like one of those car commercials you see on television; it seems so small – there's no action – and yet it's so large inside. There are so many layers there you can find if you want to.

Indeed, by any standards *Red* is a work of remarkable riches, with Kieślowski at the very peak of his powers both as writer and as director. As an examination of the notion of fraternity, it once again foregoes political comment. From its extraordinary virtuoso opening sequence, in which we see a hand dialling a phone number, before the camera traces the call's journey to its distant destination, via the lead to the plug socket, the cables that lead underground and beneath the sea, to the flashing red light in the local exchange which tells us the line is busy, it's at once apparent that the film is to be an audacious and original exploration of the hidden forces that affect communication between individuals in the modern world. Through its narrative structure and *mise en scène*, it successfully focuses attention as closely on those forces as on the human characters in the film.

Hidden forces: the virtuoso opening sequence of *Red*

THE 'THREE COLOURS' TRILOGY   53

When the caller dials again and gets through, we learn that he is Michel, the (unseen) boyfriend of Valentine (Irène Jacob), a student and part-time model living alone in Geneva. Michel has been working abroad for some time, first in Poland where he had everything stolen (echoes of *White*) and now in England; from the way he interrogates Valentine, it's clear that he's irrationally possessive, even though she tells him that in her loneliness she spent the night sleeping with his (red) jacket. As the conversation continues, intercut shots show in the street below her apartment a young man and his dog returning to a flat opposite where, as Valentine puts down her phone, the young man – a law student, we later learn, called Auguste (Jean-Pierre Lorit) – makes a call: upon hearing a woman's voice answer that he has reached a personalised weather-forecast service, he simply makes a kissing noise. Evidently, some lovers are less demanding, more trusting than Michel.

The film proceeds quickly to sketch in the contours of Valentine's life and character: in various scenes, the film shows she is a believer in chance (she plays the fruit-machine at a café called *Chez Joseph*), able to express a wide range of emotions, determined, hard-working, conscientious and kind. And, at a photo-session for a chewing-gum advertisement, in which she poses before a red drape, her expression shows there is sadness in her life.

As she drives home one night, inadvertently passing Auguste as he drops his law books on a pedestrian crossing next to a massive, empty, red-framed billboard, she collides with a dog which she immediately comforts and carries to her car. Reading its address tag and checking her map with a bloodstained finger, she drives to a large, run-down house in a secluded, hilltop garden. When no one answers her knock at the door, she enters the dark building, to be greeted by strange electronic noises (not unlike the sounds heard during the opening phone-call sequence or the interference noises that emanated from her car radio just before she hit the dog), and by the sight of an elderly man (Jean-Louis Trintignant) asleep in a chair (with a red jacket draped over it). When she wakes him to say she has brought him his injured dog, he replies, with no trace of concern, that it disappeared yesterday; accused of indifference, he tells her to leave and not to close the door (somehow knowing, without even looking round at her, that she was going to do so). Bemused and angry, she takes the dog – Rita – to the vet's, where she learns to her relief that it's merely bruised, and pregnant; for some reason, however, Valentine looks startled upon hearing the vet call her assistant's name, Marc.

Though Michel's call next morning is as jealous as its predecessor – after asking again whether she's with someone, he peremptorily tells Valentine to get rid of the dog – she is sufficiently faithful not to yield later that day to the photographer's gentle attempt to kiss her (though her hesitancy in rejecting his advances suggests her commitment to Michel is wavering). Back at the café, she wins the jackpot on the slot machine with three red cherries; though she tells the bartender she thinks she knows why she won (presumably, for her fidelity to Michel), it's not, perhaps, a good omen, in that she then sees in her newspaper a photograph of her brother Marc who, it turns out, is in trouble for his involvement with drugs. Worried, she calls him to suggest he visit their lonely, elderly mother, in case she sees the article and gets upset; evidently, Valentine likes to take responsibility for the well-being of others.

Walking Rita, she lets the dog off its (red) leash; after running into a church, it disappears. When she drives to its owner's to tell him Rita has gone missing, the dog is already in the garden. Valentine asks the man if he sent some money she received in the post; he did, as payment for the vet. But how did he know her address? 'It was easy,' is all he will say, before turning to go find her some change, and telling her to take the dog; he wants nothing. 'So stop breathing,' says Valentine; 'Good idea,' he replies, vanishing inside the house. When he fails to return, Valentine follows, only to find him entranced by banks of audio-surveillance equipment, the source of the sounds she heard before; he is listening to two men discussing their mutual love.

Already offended by his apparent indifference, Valentine is now disgusted by his admission that he spies on his neighbours. If she's so convinced that she's right, he asks, why doesn't she go tell the man who lives next door that his phone conversations are being tapped? But when

Valentine goes to do precisely that, and finds the man's young daughter also listening in, secretly, to his professions of adulterous, homosexual love, she flees the house without telling him about his spying neighbour, to whom she returns confused and shaken. Asked to put an end to his illegal activities, the man says he has done it all his life: he used to be not a cop, as she surmises, but something 'worse – a judge'.

At this point, the film embarks upon a series of scenes of sustained psychological symbiosis as the judge – *Joseph* Kern, as it transpires – and the woman try tentatively to understand one another, her innocence transformed by his wisdom, his humanity revived by her compassion. Save for a few brief, mostly wordless scenes outlining the progress of Auguste's relationship with the weather-service girl, Karin (Frédérique Feder), who by chance is also one of the judge's neighbours, much of the next half-hour takes place within the shadowy confines of Kern's retreat. As confessions are made and mysteries unfold, the mood is one of electric, claustrophobic intimacy, with Kieślowski's alternation of medium shot, two-shots and very occasional close-ups, and Preisner's sometimes ominous, purposeful bolero both serving to illuminate the tensions and the emotional inevitability of the blossoming friendship between the misanthropic recluse and his redemptive saviour.

Kern explains his reasons for spying: he feels it allows him a more truthful understanding of people than he had in his work, and prefers to remain aloof from having to make judgments about the lives of others. He also guesses the truth about Valentine's brother, who turned to drugs when he discovered, at age fifteen, that he was not in fact the son of his mother's husband; he tunes in to a call in which Auguste and Karin discuss their sex life, and tells Valentine that Auguste is yet to meet the right woman; and he shows her a man in the next-door garden who, he claims, runs Geneva's heroin trade. Suddenly seeing a potential benefit of spying, Valentine calls the man on his mobile phone to tell him he deserves to die, watching with grim satisfaction as he flees indoors, shocked by the call. Kern then tunes into a painful conversation between an ailing woman and her daughter; when Valentine is anguished by what seems to be a tale of neglect, the judge informs her that the mother is using emotional blackmail on her daughter, and asks why Valentine chose to take care of Rita – was it for the dog or for herself, to ease her guilt? Valentine objects to his cynicism – people are not bad, only weak sometimes – and leaves in tears after admitting that she pities him, and that Rita is pregnant.

Her next visit occurs, after another unpleasant call from Michel, when she sees in the paper that Kern has been prosecuted for spying. (As he waits outside the court, he sees, as potential witnesses, his various neighbours including Karin, who has just learned from Auguste that he passed his law exams by answering a question from the page at which his book fell open in the street, and who enters the courtroom deep in conversation with another man.) Valentine's reason for visiting Kern is to tell him that she didn't inform on him; of that, he says, he's already aware, since he denounced himself – he knew she would feel wrongly implicated in his arrest, and so would visit him again. When she asks why he wanted her to return, he replies that he expects something of her, and opens his arms wide; she backs away, afraid he'll make a pass, but his needs are more complex than that. He needs to unburden himself. He tells her that Auguste's and Karin's affair is nearly over, because his own

Kern unburdens himself to Valentine

eavesdropping and self-denunciation led indirectly to her meeting another man. He tells her it is both his birthday and the thirty-fifth anniversary of his having acquitted a sailor he later found out had been guilty, after which he felt that deciding what's true was an immodest act of vanity. And, when Valentine announces that she is considering abandoning her mother and brother for a trip to England (to see Michel, who has confessed that he 'thinks' he loves her, which for Valentine is not the same as actually loving someone), Kern advises her to go ('It's your destiny'), and to take a ferry rather than fly. Heartened by his friendliness, Valentine asks if he has ever loved anyone; he replies evasively that yesterday he dreamed of her, aged forty or fifty, and happy. She asks if his dreams come true; he simply says that it's years since he dreamed something nice.

Meanwhile, Auguste's phone calls to Karin are also receiving no answer. Driving past Kern's house to her apartment, he climbs up to her balcony where, through the window, he sees her making love with another man. (His view is notably more revealing than was Karol's in *White*.) Next morning he returns home so distraught that he leaves his car lights on (from her window, Valentine sees his red jeep and murmurs, 'The battery'), while the judge decides to ring Karin to enquire about

A cuckold's view: history repeats itself as Auguste watches Karin make love with another man

next week's weather in the English Channel; she tells him it will be fine, and that she's winding up her forecast service, since she's going yachting in the Channel herself. The lives of the film's four main characters are all about to change dramatically.

At a fashion-show, Valentine looks anxiously from the catwalk for the one guest she invited: Kern. Only after the show is over, as she is leaving, does he reveal himself for a final heart-to-heart in the red-upholstered theatre where, he recalls, years ago he dropped a law book; it fell open at the exact page he needed to read in order to pass his exams. He also tells her, when asked for more details of his dream, that she smiled at someone; this, he claims, will occur twenty-five years hence. Valentine is happy he has dressed up and come into town: 'I had to recharge the battery,' he replies. 'It was dead.' At which point he answers her questions about his own lost love: how as a student he found his girlfriend making love with another man. She left to go on holiday with her new lover in France and England, but died in an accident. Not only has Kern never loved anyone since – though Valentine, he confesses, is perhaps the 'right' woman he never met – but many years later, he found himself presiding over a case in which the accused was the offending seducer: initially preferring not to take the case, Kern eventually found him guilty, then, unsure of his suitability as a judge, asked for early retirement.

If I have described the contents of Valentine's conversations with the judge in detail, that is to suggest the intricacy of the many connections the narrative makes between the various characters, their surroundings, their present and past, partly because we the audience, like Kern, are led to see the parallels between his life and that of his younger counterpart, of whom, of course, Valentine herself is still unaware. Not that Kieślowski has denied us mystery or suspense. Indeed, the former is assured by the many hints Kieślowski has given us regarding Kern's prescience and seemingly 'magical' powers: during his encounters with Valentine, he predicted a sudden change in the light or seemed to influence, with the spin of a coin, Karin's arrangements to meet Auguste at a bowling alley (where, coincidentally, Valentine had been the same night as the law student). A level of taut suspense is also present throughout, due partly to the unresolved moods of Preisner's music, to Kieślowski's imaginative use of sound (the conversation in the theatre is interrupted by shocking bangs, one from a window blown open by the wind, one from a bucket dropped by an unseen cleaning lady for whom, in an echo of Kern's story, a janitor keeps searching), and to the many questions we inevitably ask ourselves about the film's outcome. Will Valentine continue her relationship with Michel, or fall for the judge, or somehow meet Auguste? Will she somehow die, like Kern's lover, on

THE 'THREE COLOURS' TRILOGY | 59

An index of selflessness: Valentine at the bottle-bank

holiday? What will happen to Karin? And does Kern really have an influence over or knowledge of the future?

As he and Valentine make their farewells outside the theatre, Kern's request to inspect the details of her (red) ferry ticket may imply that he does. Then, after he drives off into the night, Valentine notices a bent old woman struggling to deposit a bottle in a recycling bin; immediately, she goes to help. Next, we see her board the ferry, followed by Auguste and his dog; since he has only ever seen her once, on the billboard poster where he dropped his books, they still don't recognise each other, and are directed to different decks. Meanwhile, in Geneva, a torrential thunderstorm has arisen, necessitating the removal of Valentine's poster (the slogan of which – 'A breath of life'[17] – indicates her role in the judge's return to the world), and blowing over the remnants of a glass of pear brandy with which she had toasted his birthday. The tempest abated, and after celebrating Rita's having given birth to seven healthy puppies, Kern reads in his paper of a ferry disaster

Face off: a 'breath of life' becomes a tempest

in the English Channel. Turning on a television Valentine sent him by way of her brother, he watches the news report. The storm has taken its horrific toll: besides a couple on a yachting holiday (Karin and her lover?), over 1,400 ferry passengers are feared dead. So far only seven survivors have been found: Julie, the widow of a French composer; an English barman; Polish hairdresser Karol and his wife Dominique; a French citizen named Olivier; and two young Swiss by the names of Auguste and Valentine. After Kern watches the news footage of the drenched, shocked survivors, with Valentine standing next to Auguste, he smiles and goes to look, still smiling, out of his broken window, before the image returns to Valentine's face, in a composition almost identical to the 'sad' profile that graced the chewing-gum poster, and fades.

Does Kern smile merely from relief at discovering the girl is alive, or is it that his predictions – even, perhaps, his hopes or plans – have come to pass? Certainly he must be pleased that the young woman who restored his faith in humanity, who through her own faith, innocence and goodness made him care again about the outside world, has survived such a catastrophe. But since he also foresaw, and was indirectly responsible for, the presence on the ferry not only of Valentine but of Auguste, whose experiences have paralleled his own so closely that he might even be seen as Kern's alter ego or younger self, there is also surely a sense of self-satisfaction behind his smile. Indeed, to some extent Kern, not unlike Prospero in Shakespeare's *The Tempest*,[18] has been playing God. Embittered, severely disenchanted by the fickleness, injustice and sheer pain of human experience (most notably, the disappointment of his romantic life, which had left him feeling all too vulnerable), he had removed and isolated himself from any direct involvement with people or their feelings, preferring simply to observe, without judging or responding emotionally to their chaotic, complicated lives. However, his peculiarly detailed knowledge (derived from his surveillance equipment) of how those lives intersect and influence each other also bestowed on him an almost God-like power which, in his indifference, he refrained from using. Only when Valentine touched his heart, reviving memories of his youthful love, and inspiring him with her almost wholly selfless behaviour, did he decide to abandon his aloof, voyeuristic ways and intervene in people's lives, by untangling, as it were, the crossed wires of their relationships with each other. And in becoming an active, sentient, responsible being once more, by putting aside and learning to accept the mistakes and disappointments of his own past, he has been reborn.

If Kern 'is' God, however, he is neither omnipotent nor even omniscient; while he may influence the destiny of others, free will and blind chance – be it a slot-machine, a dog run over by a car, or stormy weather – still play a major part in shaping individual lives. Rather, Kern seems to 'direct' people, as if they were characters in a script which he then tweaks and turns into a finished film. Initially a voyeur reluctant to participate in the stories he observes going on around him, the judge later elects to manipulate people's lives towards what he would like to think is a neat, satisfactory outcome. To some extent, then, Kern may even be seen as some kind of self-portrait by Kieślowski.

In which case, it is easy to see why the film's ending is so very moving: a neat, satisfactory outcome in itself, perhaps, as long as we acknowledge certain important qualifications. While we are glad to see Valentine and Auguste safe and together at last, and to see Kern smile, it would, I think, be cynical or short-sighted to describe the outcome of *Red* in simplistic terms as 'a happy ending'. For one thing, it is far from certain that Valentine and Auguste will, as Kern's dream suggested, spend the rest of their lives together, let alone that they'll be happy; for another, we should not forget that the price of their finally being brought together is over 1,400 lives, including, it is implied, those of Auguste's former girlfriend and his dog. Rather, what makes the conclusion emotionally satisfying is the compassion extended, not only by Kern to Valentine and a reflection of his younger self, but by Kieślowski himself to the major characters of the entire trilogy. Seeing the protagonists of *Blue* and *White* take their place as survivors alongside those of *Red*, we are not only given hope regarding their (hitherto ambiguous) futures, but we may somehow feel that we the audience have been rewarded by Kieślowski for taking a sympathetic interest in their fates.

(Overleaf) Destiny and compassion: Valentine survives catastrophe to face another day

62 | BFI MODERN CLASSICS

THE 'THREE COLOURS' TRILOGY | 63

There is also, of course, the sense that Kern too faces a brighter future, not only because Valentine has breathed life back into him, but because – if we accept that Auguste is, in some way, a younger surrogate for the judge – what Kieślowski called 'a mistake in time' has been rectified. (In this regard, *Red*, like *Blind Chance* and, to some extent, *The Double Life of Véronique*, is a 'what if' film, in the conditional mood.) Kern himself not only lost his first great love, but feels himself too old, upon getting to know Valentine, to court a woman he wishes he had met years before. Now, however, he may be able to derive vicarious pleasure from the knowledge that she has met Auguste.[19]

Again, Kieślowski's brilliance in assembling the various elements of the film to achieve lucid, eloquent expression is evident throughout. Even more than in *Blue*, the performances in *Red* are of an amazing intensity. Irène Jacob exudes a radiance and simplicity that underline Valentine's selfless kindness and moral integrity, even as her shy mannerisms, quiet, hesitant speech and faintly puzzled facial expressions hint at her innocence, vulnerability and confusion. Jean-Louis Trintignant, meanwhile, is fully her equal, his sullen stare, terse responses to her questions, and unenergetic gait conveying Kern's initial lack of

Free to feel for others: Kern's mysterious smile

enthusiasm for life, while his increasingly relaxed gestures and smiles signal the warmth he feels from his regeneration.

At the same time, both script and direction judiciously allow the overall intensity of the film to lower with occasional moments of nicely-judged humour: Rita's rush into a church, the drug-dealer's mystified panic at being called by a menacing stranger, the judge's various eccentricities – absent-mindedly pouring a kettle on to his carpet, or inviting Valentine to snap his braces because 'it makes a lovely noise'. But what's most impressive is Kieślowski's expertise in using sound, image and editing to clarify the many ways in which his characters' lives are interlinked: through, once more, a reference to the composer Van den Budenmayer (who figures both in a portrait on Kern's desk and in an evocative record-store scene in which the customers, including Valentine and Auguste who both want to buy a Van den Budenmayer CD, stand together, lost in their own separate worlds as they listen to headphones); and through the many echoes and rhymes in the narrative. Sound, especially, is used almost subliminally to suggest the workings of something which may justifiably be called destiny: the first view of Auguste (both for us and, unwittingly, for Valentine) is accompanied, somewhat bizarrely, by the whirring of helicopters, which we certainly don't see or expect to be flying over Geneva, but which we do hear again after the ferry disaster. Similarly, at Valentine's photo-shoot, at the very moment when, having been told to think of something sad, she hits the pose and expression that will not only feature on the chewing-gum poster but be echoed in the final shot of her having survived the ferry disaster, we inexplicably hear the sound of a ship's horn; either Kieślowski is suggesting that, in imagining something sad, she has some premonition of what will befall her, or he is once more pointing, by way of a small omen she herself doesn't even notice, to the mysterious, hidden forces that determine our fate. Likewise ambiguous but suggestive of destiny is the way the interference on Valentine's car radio – which causes her to collide with Rita – sounds very like, and is quite possibly produced by, the electronic sounds of Kern's surveillance system; at the very least, the noise is a contributory factor in bringing Valentine and the judge together, although there may also be a hint that he is somehow using the sounds to 'call' the girl to him.

But Kieślowski also creates links between his characters' lives through the ubiquitous but subtly controlled use of the colour red – for rocking-chairs, cars, bed-linen, stop-lights, dance-studios, dog-leads, jackets, café canopies, bowling balls, rescue-workers' uniforms and so forth. At the same time, however, it has a resonance over and beyond any such connections, since red is the colour of danger, blood, warmth, passion and, perhaps most importantly here, the life force.

6 The Trilogy: Connections

The *Three Colours* trilogy takes Kieślowski a long way from Poland's 'Cinema of Moral Anxiety' (generally held to have arisen in 1976 with Wajda's *Man of Marble* and Zanussi's *Camouflage*, and to have ended with Bugajski's *The Interrogation* in 1981) in its accounts of freedom, equality and fraternity and lack of concern with political awareness. Indeed, as a whole the trilogy focuses on love, compassion, and the way lives may be influenced by destiny, free will and chance. As Kieślowski put it:

> I think we're fighting our own fate, our own destiny, all the time. There is something like fate, but there is also our resistance to it; and perhaps that's the reason for our suffering, our feeling of not having fulfilled ourselves. ... But I am not a fatalist; I don't think that everything's written up in black and white in advance.

This, and his statement, 'All my films are about individuals who can't quite find their bearings, who don't quite know how to live ... and are desperately looking,'[20] are fitting descriptions of what the trilogy is 'about'. Each *Three Colours* film focuses on a solitary character or characters who are inherently 'good' but who have somehow, due to a traumatic change in their lives, lost their way: for Julie and Kern, the trauma comes from the chance loss of a loved one; for Karol it is also the

Dominique sauvée des eaux: surviving through chance, destiny, or a director's compassion?

loss of his confidence and potency. Each, in different ways, loses his or her faith in 'normal' human compassion; each, too, needs to regain that faith and rediscover love – whether sexual or platonic – as a *modus vivendi* in order to regain some sense of equilibrium, happiness and shared humanity. A crucial step, for each, is to learn from the errors and disappointments of the past, and then to set aside the past so that they may get on with living out the present. (Memories should be neither fetishised nor ignored.) That, however, is not easy, as Kieślowski himself acknowledged: 'There's a need within us ... to believe that those who have gone and whom we dearly loved, who were important to us, are constantly within and around us. ... We take their opinions into account even though they're not there any more, even though they're dead.'[21] In other words, in trying to find our way through life, we need to come to terms with the workings of fate, chance, the past, ghosts, maybe even God – things unseen, one and all.

In this respect, Kieślowski belongs to that small number of filmmakers – most notable are Dreyer, Rossellini, Bresson, Bergman and Tarkovsky – who have attempted to explore, through a medium that is by its very nature materialistic and confined to the visual reproduction of physical surfaces, a world that is obscure, metaphysical and transcendental. (Nevertheless, it is important to note that Kieślowski differed from Bresson and Rossellini in not being a Catholic, and from the Lutheran-raised Bergman in not being anguished, it seems, by the 'silence' of God.)[22] While refusing ever to describe himself as 'Religious with a capital R' – he hated organised religion – he would, if pressed, admit to being 'religious' only in that, 'I do think something exists beyond this ashtray, this glass, this microphone'. And while Kieślowski fully deserves to be acclaimed as a humanist, as a chronicler of contemporary mores, as an expert storyteller and an accomplished technician, it was, first and foremost, his ability to evoke those mysterious, unseen forces and our reactions to them, that made him one of the greatest film-makers in the history of the cinema.

Crucial to Kieślowski's method, in this regard, was his determination to root his stories within a recognisable, material world: in short, the metaphysical is incarnated by the physical. Rather than use fuzzily romantic 'holy' images to portray epiphanies or transcendental experiences in the Hollywood tradition of films like those of Cecil B. DeMille or *The Song of Bernardette* (Henry King, 1943), the *Three Colours* films suggest the presence of the extraordinary or inexplicable by showing something that is ordinary or familiar in itself, in a *context* which is extraordinary or inexplicable. Music or a light may suddenly appear, unexpectedly, as if from nowhere; a coin may seem to defy the law of gravity; off-screen sounds may suggest a life beyond what we can see on screen. Even Kieślowski's camera, which tends to focus only on what is 'essential' to the film's meaning, may seem to take on a life of its own, hovering in a room so that a character seems strangely aware of and unsettled by its presence (*Blue*), or darting about to inspect objects while mirroring no point of view except its own (*Red*). At the same time, such techniques are not deployed self-consciously to draw attention to the virtuosity of the film-making, but to convey information as precisely and evocatively as possible. Kieślowski never appears to have been interested in style for style's sake; likewise, then, while compositions may sometimes be imaginatively lit, colour-filtered or even 'distorted' through, say, a short lens to emphasise a particular character or object in the frame, his images are never merely prettily picturesque, but resonant with meaning.

The narratives, too, can seem mysterious, not only because of their often elliptical construction, which allows the audience to piece them together only gradually, but because they are filled with odd coincidences, repetitions, parallels and connections. The topography of the immaterial and abstract – whether it be the individual soul, or the workings of destiny and chance – is explored, as it were, in the spaces that exist *between* images. It is almost as if Kieślowski had taken to heart Robert Bresson's dictum that 'Each shot is like a word, meaning nothing in itself … it is lent meaning by its context' – except of course that, as we have seen, in Kieślowski's films simpler, physical meanings also exist within individual images.

Nevertheless, it is primarily through the connections he makes, both within individual films *and* between one film and another, that we are able to grasp the full implications of his work. In the trilogy, not only do all the main characters end up as survivors of the ferry disaster in *Red*, but Julie from *Blue* is briefly spotted entering (by mistake) the courtroom where Karol's and Dominique's case is being heard at the start of *White*, while Dominique and Karol can be seen, even more briefly, outside the courtroom at the end of *Blue*. Other such links between the three films include the different, telling reactions of Julie, Karol and Valentine to the struggles of elderly people at bottle banks, and the use of the music of Van den Budenmayer in both *Blue* and *Red*.[23] These various correspondences are not mere window-dressing designed to render more decorative otherwise straightforward stories (although Kieślowski did regard the repeated references in his work to the fictional dead composer partly as a joke); their existence and the ways in which they interconnect are part and parcel of the trilogy's concern with chance, destiny and shared humanity. This is exemplified in the magnificent ending in which six of the trilogy's main characters are survivors of the ferry disaster. The director explained how the idea came about:

It was always my intention to bring all the characters together in the last scene. The intention was similar to that of *The Decalogue*, and boils down to a very

Crossed wires and brief encounters: Julie wanders into *White*

simple concept: that the life of every single person is interesting if you just look at it. In *The Decalogue*, they all lived on one estate; we looked behind various windows and told the stories we found there. With the trilogy, a few people are saved from the ferry, so let's see who they are, how they live, and perhaps even find out why they were on the ferry.

There is, however, a crucial difference between the device as used in *The Decalogue* and the trilogy: whereas in the former the housing estate was a continuous presence from the very first episode, the ferry makes its appearance only in the trilogy's final sequence, a structural choice on Kieślowski's part with several repercussions (he could, presumably, have begun with the disaster and then used flashbacks to tell the characters' various stories). First, and most obviously, placing the disaster at the very end, as opposed to the beginning, means that the audience is left uncertain as to what will happen to the characters; until we learn of its occurence and see who survived, we have no real idea of what will become of them. Second, by situating the news of their survival at the end, Kieślowski closes his trilogy – much of which has concerned loss, grief, solitude and despair – on a note of hope: they are alive, and together. Third, the catastrophe (and the lead characters' good fortunes

An index of self-pity: Karol at the bottle-bank

in surviving it) is not unlike a *deus ex machina* in a Greek tragedy, and consequently points up the author's own artifice in giving us an emotionally satisfying outcome to all that has gone before. Finally, and most importantly, whereas the relationship of the housing estate to *The Decalogue* was structurally *aetiological* (i.e. causal), the ferry disaster's relationship to the *Three Colours* films is essentially *teleological*: everything in the trilogy works towards the catastrophe, evoking a sense of purpose or destiny.

There are structural parallels, too, between the three films: each foregrounds, as a plot device, a different mode of travel (by land, air and sea respectively); each concerns, in part, the development of a new friendship (Julie with Lucille, Karol with Mikolaj, Kern with Valentine) and the delayed gratification of a sexual relationship; each ends with a reversal of fortune and a sad smile. With the trilogy, Kieślowski achieved that rare, remarkable fusion, where the elements of form and content are so immaculately and imaginatively interwoven throughout, and so perfectly in harmony with each other, that they finally become inseparable; style never seems to have been arbitrarily imposed on the subject matter, but to have arisen organically from it. And, I would argue, it is in that respect that the *Three Colours* trilogy constitutes Kieślowski's greatest achievement.

7 The Trilogy: Reflections

Though Kieślowski spoke openly of his admiration for many writers (notably the Greek tragedians, Shakespeare, Dostoevsky, Kafka, Camus and Vargas Llosa) and for certain film-makers (Welles, Fellini, Bergman, Tarkovsky and Loach),[24] and while one should not discount the effects of his having worked closely at times with Polish film-makers such as Zanussi, Wajda and Holland, as an artist he was very much an individual, with his own cinematic style and thematic preoccupations. The *Three Colours* trilogy constitutes his finest achievement as a film-maker, being seen, both individually and collectively, as continuations and refinements of his earlier work. Not only did he himself regard his fiction features as something of a logical development from his documentary work (in that they were primarily concerned with ideas rather than 'action'), but many elements in his last three films had already appeared, in a different form or context, in the features that preceded them.

Just as the ferry disaster develops upon the use of a Warsaw housing estate in *The Decalogue*, so the trilogy's use of three old people struggling to deposit bottles in recycling bins, as an index of Julie, Karol and Valentine's compassion for others, was to some extent anticipated by *The Decalogue*'s casting of the actor Artur Barcís (in all but episodes 7 and 10) as different, unnamed characters who for the most part simply observe, at key points in the narrative, the actions of the various protagonists. But *The Decalogue* was not alone in anticipating the trilogy's sense of separate, seemingly unconnected lives touching one another briefly and by chance: just as, for example, two main characters from *Decalogue 2* make a fleeting appearance in *Decalogue 5 (A Short Film About Killing)*, so lives intersect in *The Double Life of Véronique* (where the notion of interlinked destinies informs the film's prime subject matter) and in *Blind Chance* (whose tryptych form presages, on a smaller scale, the trilogy itself). Presentiments and omens, too, recur throughout Kieślowski's work, most notably in *No End*, *Decalogue 1* and *Véronique*, while Kieślowski and Preisner's fictional Dutch composer Van den Budenmayer is also a carry-over from earlier work: 'his' music was sung and taught in *Véronique*, and the poignant song heard in *Red* had already been introduced to *Decalogue 9*'s doctor protagonist by a singer with a heart complaint (again cf. *Véronique*). (Intriguingly, the doctor, like Kern and Auguste, was to suffer the painful indignity of witnessing his beloved's infidelity; on the soundtrack CD for *Red* the song is listed under the title 'Do Not Take Another Man's Wife'.)

More specifically, *Blue* develops on scenes and themes in *Decalogue 3* (an elderly woman in a nursing home believes that her grown niece is still a child); *Decalogue 6 (A Short Film About Love)* (the difficulty of living without love); *Véronique* (a girl 'visited' by mysterious lights evocative of a supernatural presence); and *No End*, which concerns a woman's attempts to come to terms with the death of her lawyer husband (visible to the audience as a ghost). *White*, meanwhile, reworks the notion of the painful impossibility of equality in love from *Decalogue 6*; the links between impotence, insecurity and infidelity from *Decalogue 9*; the story of a man awaiting the release of his lover from prison from *Blind Chance*; and the darkly comic portrait of a criminally materialistic Poland where everything can be bought (here, a kidney rather than an entire corpse) from *Decalogue 10*, which like *White* also starred, as brothers, Jerzy Stuhr (who had already appeared for Kieślowski in *The Scar*, *The Calm* and *Camera Buff*) and Zbigniew Zamachowski.

A (non-existent) artist revealed: Van den Budenmayer in *Red*

Finally, *Red* includes numerous variants on moments, motifs and themes from Kieślowski's earlier films. The plane explosion that closes *Blind Chance* prefigures the ferry disaster; *No End* and *Decalogue 5* anticipate Kern's disillusionment with the legal system; *Decalogue 1* and *2* both allude to dead dogs (the second run over by a car), while the latter centres on a lonely doctor haunted by the loss of his family and tempted to play God in a way not unlike Kern. *Decalogue 4* concerns a 'mistake in time' relationship between a middle-aged man and a younger woman; *Decalogue 6* features voyeurism; *Decalogue 8* includes a portrait of a woman remarkable for her selfless willingness to take responsibility for others; while *Véronique* foregrounds parallel lives, doubles, the workings of destiny, and a character who manipulates the actions of others through his technical expertise with sound-recording equipment.

It should be clear, then, that as with many other great film-makers, such as Renoir, Ozu, Hawks, Bresson, Rohmer and Fassbinder, Kieślowski's artistry was partly a matter of reworking, re-evaluating and refining, over and over again, certain key elements of what might be called his 'world-view'. As his career progressed, and his cinematic style became ever more confident and sophisticated, his world-view became more complex, culminating in the immensely rich, impressively detailed

The perils of film-making: Jerzy Stuhr (who later played Jurek in *White*) as the amateur auteur in *Camera Buff*

tapestry of the *Three Colours* trilogy. By the end of the trilogy, Kieślowski's attitude to life was both clear and complex: we all of us live in a world tainted by grief, loneliness and suffering, and the only way to achieve some sort of equilibrium or 'spiritual' peace is by acknowledging the fact that we share that desire for a fuller, happier life with the rest of mankind. In order to satisfy our most fundamental needs, we must not allow ourselves to become overly concerned either with what seem to be the dictates of the past (which is valuable only insofar as experience enables us to learn from past errors) or with ourselves. We must reach out to others, through love, compassion and understanding, and we should accept that there are bonds between us which we may not fully comprehend; to recognise our common humanity, our equal worth as individuals with our own special needs, desires, fears and responsibilities, is to accept our 'destiny'. Only by accepting the mysteries of existence for what they are can we proceed towards a greater understanding of ourselves and others, unfettered by any notions of ideological or moral absolutes.

Though the trilogy was Kieślowski's most sophisticated, subtle and profoundly personal expression of these attitudes, to the astonishment of many, he announced that *Red* would be his last film as director; he was, he said, tired of the day-to-day grind of making movies. Nevertheless, disappointed by this news as his admirers may have been, few were in any doubt as to the fact that the trilogy was the perfect valedictory work with which to end a distinguished career.

8 The Trilogy: Coda

In terms of its reception by critics and cinemagoers alike, the *Three Colours* trilogy was, by art-movie standards, enormously successful. At its première at the Venice Film Festival, *Blue* shared the Golden Lion for Best Film with Robert Altman's *Short Cuts*, while also receiving the Best Actress award for Juliette Binoche and the Best Photography award for Slawomir Idziak; in Berlin, *White* won Kieślowski the Silver Bear for Best Director.

Only *Red*, at its première in Cannes, failed to win a major prize (the *Palme d'Or* went to *Pulp Fiction*, whose director Quentin Tarantino described Kieślowski's film as 'a masterpiece'); and that was seen by many as a serious error of judgment on the part of the jury, or, more seriously, as a political move designed to deny the director the first ever 'grand slam' of winning major awards at Europe's three most prestigious film festivals. All the same, the films, especially *Blue* and *Red*, performed very well at the box-office and garnered, for the most part, enthusiastic reviews, with critics praising both their ambition and execution. Fairly typical of the favourable notices, for example, were Nigel Andrews' view in the *Financial Times* review of *Blue*, that 'Kieślowski's genius – and he may be the only European director now earning that word – is for shuffling his deck of images so that animate and inanimate become indistinguishable'; Geoff Brown's opinion in *The Times* that *White* was 'black, scathing East European comedy ... abrasive yet humane film-making, and a joy to behold'; or Lisa Nesselson's assessment of *Red* in *Variety*: '... another deft, deeply affecting variation on Krzysztof Kieślowski's recurring theme that people are interconnected in ways they can barely fathom. ... Narrative has a purposeful randomness – the viewer is assured via countless subtle details that the story is ineluctably headed toward something faintly ominous and cathartic. Denouement and final image are a satisfying grace note both to this film and the entire trilogy.'

Disappointments expressed by the more serious film critics tended to fall into two camps: claims that the trilogy was too 'arty' and lacked the edge of his earlier, more political Polish films; and complaints that the director's elliptical storytelling style had taken a turn for the worse in rendering many of his characters' motivations obscure and unintelligible. In the *Guardian*, for example, Derek Malcolm opined that because *White* dealt with Poles and Poland and was 'less headily stylish' than *Blue* or *Red*, 'it feels somehow truer, as if the director instinctively knows how his characters should react and can thus afford a more direct, less elliptical approach', while *The Times*' Geoff Brown complained that the characters in *Blue* were 'impenetrable ciphers ... the film appears icy, remote. We remain on the outside, looking in, admiring the artistry, feeling nothing'.

Clearly, the charge that Kieślowski's move away from the more political content of his Polish films entailed a shift into an excessive concern with style comes down to a question of personal preference. My own view is that Kieślowski's 'artiness' simply lay in his attempts to use film's various 'signifying codes' (script, performance, camera movement, composition, colour, lighting, cutting, music, sound, etc.) to express his ideas as eloquently and exactly as possible. The shift away from political subjects, too, towards questions that may perhaps be described as more humanist and spiritual seemed to bring with it a more complex, sophisticated, all-embracing grasp of the many diverse factors that affect and influence the actions and experiences of the individual, particularly as Kieślowski still showed an interest in his characters' relationships with the world around them. As for the second criticism, that his stories and characters had become 'colder' and more 'impenetrable', I hope that my earlier analyses have demonstrated that the trilogy is anything but obscure or unintelligible. Certainly, Kieślowski's close and detailed attention to the psychological and emotional needs of his characters is motivated by a warm, unsentimental affection for them as sentient, intelligent human beings; the intimacy of his approach, far from making them 'ciphers', is firm evidence of his desire to understand, in the fullest possible sense of the word, their deepest emotions, thoughts and actions.

Nevertheless, it is perhaps interesting to speculate on why Kieślowski's later work was viewed, in some quarters, with a degree of grudging admiration sometimes bordering on downright suspicion. There is no question that Kieślowski was, during the late 80s and early 90s, one of the most visible practitioners of what may be described, for want of a better term, as the European art-movie. To some extent, the art-movie tradition, so critically respected in the 60s and early 70s, had fallen into disrepute. By the 80s, Hollywood's hegemony of the movie world was stronger than ever, so that 'foreign-language' movies were increasingly marginalised both in terms of exhibition and distribution, and in terms of the attention paid to them by the media. Worse, Hollywood itself had come to rely more and more on spectacular action-movies, distinguished primarily by their use of state-of-the-art technology and gimmicky, escapist storylines which had little or nothing to do with serious socio-political, moral, psychological or philosophical questions relating to the everyday lives of 'ordinary' people. As a result, the art-movie came to be widely regarded as somehow redundant, especially after the death, retirement or commercial decline of once big-name auteurs like Truffaut, Tarkovsky, Bergman, Fellini, Bresson, Buñuel, Godard, Wenders, Fassbinder and Pasolini. There was a widespread assumption that the art-movie tradition was moribund, and that the few auteurs still mining the vein of modernist or humanist high-art – people like Michelangelo Antonioni, Theo Angelopoulos, Jacques Rivette, Chris Marker, Joao Botelho and even the Taviani Brothers – were fundamentally irrelevant,

'Animate and inanimate become indistinguishable' (Nigel Andrews): Valentine's poster in *Red*

wasting both their time and ours. The critical and commercial standing of the European art-movie were at their lowest for decades, and when Kieślowski began to move away from his documentaries and more political work towards the more complex, polished and 'spiritual' films of his later years, he to some extent found himself tarred with the same brush, viewed with the same suspicion as those other neglected film-makers mentioned above. Which is not to say that critics, or indeed audiences, did not enjoy or applaud his work; merely that, the art-movie having a somewhat elitist reputation, they were perhaps a little wary of attributing too much import to Kieślowski's challenging, thought-provoking films.

It may be that Kieślowski himself was aware of this scepticism and resistance, since with *The Decalogue* and the *Three Colours* trilogy he adopted a production strategy pioneered by Eric Rohmer, whose decision to present his films as part of the *Contes moraux*, *Comédies et proverbes* and *Contes des quatre saisons* series was motivated not only by financial concerns but by the recognition that viewers might more readily understand and accept his delicately detailed exploration of human psychology if they were given repeated opportunities to become acquainted with his miniaturist methods. Certainly, working in the series format brought Kieślowski his greatest commercial success, allowing him to reach a wider audience than previously; crucially, it also, as we have seen, allowed him to explore his ideas with ever greater complexity and freedom, by forging and making use of thematic and narrative links between individual films. And it is through those subtly detailed connections that one may best comprehend and appreciate both his purpose and his magnificent achievement.

There is a great wealth of subtly detailed 'information' in the three films of the trilogy, making it almost impossible to do proper justice to their complexity in a book of this length; each frame and every line of dialogue are resonant with meaning, offering more and more riches with repeated screenings. If, after reading this book, readers return to the trilogy to discover new facets of Kieślowski's genius for themselves, it will have achieved its purpose.

9 Elegy: Remembering Kieślowski

I had the good fortune to interview Kieślowski twice: the 'official' agenda of our encounters was to discuss *Blue* and *Red*, but by the time of the second meeting, he had already announced his retirement, and I took the opportunity to ask a few more general questions about his career and, more specifically, why he felt the need to bring it to an end. As during our first meeting (when we both, though nursing terrible colds, sat chain-smoking quite happily), he was courteous, patient and thoughtful in his responses to what may have seemed faintly impertinent questions. (It must have become clear, very early on, that I was trying to persuade him to resume his career – after, of course, a much-needed rest.) But then, notwithstanding the common assumption that, in interviews at least, he was forbiddingly serious, dour, even cantankerous, Kieślowski turned out, to my relief and pleasure, to be a warm, gracious, enormously likeable person, blessed with a dry, ironic, frequently self-deprecating wit, an appealing modesty and a great sense of human compassion. Though a printed interview can never properly convey the nuances of delivery, let alone the flavour of the speaker's personality, I hope that some of these qualities emerge from the following edited transcript of that conversation.

GA: In *Blue* you seem to be suggesting that musical composition is a matter of inspiration; that musical ideas come out of the ether and that artistic creativity is partly a question of being open to them. Do you feel that's also true of film-making?

KK: In music, yes, it's simply a matter of drawing such things in. But film is different from music; I regard myself as a storyteller. Film *can* be an art, but has been, unfortunately, only rarely. Literature's different, but then that's existed far longer. Maybe the problem is that we haven't had time yet. And I don't think we will have time, because something – I don't know what – will take the place of film.

GA: Nevertheless, you would surely agree that you have tried to explore what might be called the spiritual, immaterial world – even if you've had to do it by focusing on the physical world?

KK: But film is very materialistic: all you can photograph, most of the time, is *things*. You can describe a soul, but you can't photograph it; you have to find an equivalent. But there isn't really an equivalent. Film is helpless when it comes to describing the soul, just as it is describing many other things, like a state of consciousness. You have to find methods, tricks, which may be more or less successful in making it understood that this is what your film is about. And some people may like those tricks, others may not.

I'm frustrated by the literalism of film; I'd like to escape that. To a certain degree, maybe I have managed to do so in the last few films, but only to a certain degree. And now I can't find any more possibilities; the camera is of no help. So that's one reason I'd like to give up filmmaking.

GA: Do you feel pessimistic about the future of cinema?

KK: (*laughing*) I'm a pessimist about everything! And film clearly has a place in that.

I don't watch many movies; I don't rush to see anyone's new film. But I did like two English films recently: *Raining Stones* and *The Snapper*. I watched them because I had to, as a duty, but it was a pleasure. I saw that it was still possible to do something that used to be possible; Loach and Frears knew that people are interested in their neighbours' lives, and that simple people can be shown. That's touching. And it's pleasing, too, that you can still make that sort of low-budget film and make some return on it.

GA: You always describe yourself as a pessimist, but aren't your more recent films touched with a kind of transcendent optimism?

KK: Yes, there is something like that. It's probably connected with my trying to move closer to the individual. I really think that there's more hope in individual people than in the social and political principles that rule our lives; that each of us has, within ourselves, some sort of basis that is good. But at the same time, even with that, we create a world that is bad. It's strange: the world is evil and stupid.

GA: Is that because, as soon as one individual becomes involved with another, some sort of power struggle comes into play?

KK: Yes: competitiveness, power struggles. But I don't know the answers to all the questions I pose. I'm not even sure whether I formulate the questions correctly, but I certainly don't know the answers. And since I don't know the answers myself, it would be unfair to lay them out for other people.

GA: Can you explain more fully the reasons for your decision to retire from directing?

KK: After making the trilogy, without any real breaks in the filming, I'm tired. Tiredness is written into the profession. I'm also impatient, and patience is absolutely necessary for a director; everyone else on set can be impatient, but not the director. So I have to pretend I'm patient when really I'm not. And I just don't want to pretend any more. You need patience for everything: the weather, the moods of the director of photography, the actors – everything. You're constantly waiting for something, and nothing turns out exactly the way you'd like it. So I've lost my patience little by little, and now I haven't got it any more.

'Each of us has, within ourselves, some sort of basis that is good' (Kieślowski): Valentine in *Red*

GA: But what if an idea came up that you really liked? Would you return to film-making then?

KK: No. The reason I say I won't make any more films is so that I won't make them. I've set a trap for myself, consciously.

GA: Couldn't you perhaps write?

KK: You need talent to write, which I don't have.

GA: Many would disagree.

KK: (*smiling*) I can't help that.

GA: But some of us have been profoundly affected by your films; they clarify things for us. You've already spoken about the fifteen-year-old girl in Paris who went to see *Véronique* several times and told you that it had made her realise there was such a thing as the soul. And you said it was worth making films for people like her.[25]

KK: Yes, that's why I do it. But you can't foresee that. You might want it but not attain it. And as you well know, 99 per cent of people don't feel like that. So yes, that's my intention, but it's just ... (*a smile*) wishful thinking.

GA: Do you have any regrets regarding your career?

KK: No. I think I've achieved more than I thought I would. I've met the right people in my professional life – in my private life, too, of course – and I've never actually had to make a film I didn't want to make. That's not true for many directors; usually they have to make at least one thing they don't like, for some reason or another. But if you ask whether I've made all the films I'd have liked to ... probably not. But I don't feel any great loss because of that.

GA: Do you attribute that freedom to your having worked mainly in Poland, for a state-funded industry?

KK: Yes; but then when I came to the West, I still made what I wanted to!

GA: You've said that upon retiring you intend to return to live in Poland – yet in *White* you portray the country in a pretty unpleasant light. So why do you want to return?

KK: Actually, I've already returned there. And it's unpleasant, but it's my place. If something is your own, you're entitled to have a critical opinion of it, more so than of things that aren't yours. You can be very critical of your own wife, less so of your friend's wife. Of the people we love, we demand and expect more; it's the same with places. For me, England can be as it likes, but Poland I'd like to be different. It's never the way I'd like it to be, but I have the right to those expectations. It's awful, but it's mine! And I couldn't live anywhere else. I like Paris, and lived there a few years, but I couldn't live there forever.

GA: So how do you plan to live, what do you plan to do in Poland?

KK: I've put a bit of money aside; not much, but enough. I don't have any great needs. I live in Warsaw, but I have a house in the country, and I try to be in the country as often as I can. It's nicer there ... and there's no telephone!

But I don't have any specific plans. Making films isn't a proper way to live; if you really want a life, you really have to *live* and not make films. So my real ambition is to live normally. No plans – with films you have to make plans, know what you're going to be making in the next

Joseph Kern in *Red*: a portrait of the artist?

year or two, sort out getting the actors and editing rooms at the right time. In normal life, you don't have or need such plans; you don't know what will happen tomorrow, let alone in a year or so's time. And that's the difference.

Sadly, of course, Krzysztof Kieślowski didn't know what would happen in a year or so's time; his attempts to return to a less tiring, calmer, more 'normal' existence were tragically short-lived. Like Joseph Kern in *Red*, he had grown increasingly tired of his profession (which, he told me, he didn't feel was a 'very honourable' one); also like Kern, however, he had emerged from it with his principles and compassion intact. We shall never know for sure whether his retirement from film-making would have been permanent. Only months before his death, it was announced that he and Piesiewicz were planning to start work on another trilogy of films, provisionally entitled *Heaven*, *Hell* and *Purgatory*. (At the time, Irène Jacob, who had remained in contact with Kieślowski, believed that

'I've achieved more than I thought I would': Krzysztof Kieślowski (1941–1996)

he intended only to write the films and oversee their production; as originally planned for *The Decalogue*, he would probably hand over the task of direction to three young film-makers.) It was not to be, however. Fate not only deprived cinemagoers of three movies whose very titles suggested that Kieślowski's considerable ambitions remained undiminished, but robbed the film-making world of one of its most remarkable practitioners. His talents, surely, will be missed. But his films live on, as a testament to his humanity and integrity, and to his ability to make us feel, and look at the world afresh.

Notes

1 Danusia Stok (ed.), *Kieślowski on Kieślowski* (London: Faber and Faber, 1993), pp. 210–11.
2 Ibid., p. 5.
3 Ibid., p. 55.
4 Ibid., p. 39.
5 Ibid., p. 113.
6 Ibid., p. 130.
7 Ibid., p. 143.
8 Jonathan Romney, '*La Double vie de Véronique*', *Sight and Sound*, March 1992.
9 Stok, *Kieślowski on Kieślowski*, pp. 193–4.
10 Kieślowski makes so little of the fact that the concerto was commissioned to commemorate the Unification of Europe that it is hard to deduce any political implications from this detail. Certainly it reflects the mood of the times in which the film was made, and it may also cast light on Patrice's real status as a 'serious' composer; if he is acclaimed, in death, as a great artist both by patriotic funeral orators and, presumably, by the Eurocrats who commissioned the work, that suggests merely that he was known for popular, accessible anthems rather than original, adventurous compositions. At the same time, of course, the notion of Unification is in keeping with the film's final celebration of love and shared humanity.
11 Stok, *Kieślowski on Kieślowski*, pp. 34–5.
12 Kieślowski himself regarded his choice of this particular pendant as a mistake: 'Having been brought up in a Catholic country, and being opposed to its religious institutions, I was really an idiot to choose a crucifix on a chain for the prop, when I could have chosen a little apple or heart.'
13 Though the bizarre television footage (repeated again later) of men – one of them very old – performing various risky aerial feats certainly enhances the melancholy mood of this scene, it would seem to have no particular relevance to the film's overall meaning. Kieślowski informed me that it was intended merely as a little joke, born of the fact that wherever he went in the world, the televisions he switched on in various hotel rooms always seemed to be showing ridiculous programmes of ordinary people subjecting themselves to humiliation, indignity or danger.
14 There are hints that for Julie, Lucille – arguably the film's most 'innocent' character in so far as, like a child, she happily goes about without underwear and naively believes that anyone would, like her, enjoy exposing their naked body to the public gaze – perhaps comes to represent a surrogate daughter-figure. As a child, Lucille says, she owned and loved a blue chandelier like the one in Julie's flat – which Julie, in her desire to keep her past a private secret, tells Lucille she 'found'.

It is also, perhaps, interesting to note how largely broken or dysfunctional families loom in Kieślowski's work. Parents are often left single, whether by divorce or death; children, if they see their parents at all, are frequently troubled by the relationship. While the *Three Colours* films focus on individuals rather than families *per se*, Kieślowski clearly felt that the contemporary family unit was in some sort of crisis, for which the trilogy's emphasis on love as a healing force might even be seen as a kind of prescription or cure for contemporary ills.
15 It is difficult, I think, to deduce any particular sinister or perverse motivation behind Olivier's purchase of the mattress. Though perhaps an unusual act, it is a sentimental one born of his love for Julie; unlike her, he is ready and able to live with his memories and his feelings for others, and

accepts the truth of the past.

16 Kieślowski was adamant that the text from Corinthians should not be interpreted in a purely Christian sense: 'It was consciously chosen as the only text in the Bible which doesn't speak of God; it says that love is more important than faith. We could have chosen other songs or poems about love, but this fragment showed that people have always thought this way, even 2,000 years ago; if I live without love, I am nothing.'

17 The French phrase on the poster, 'Fraîcheur de vivre', literally means 'freshness of life', echoing the way Valentine refreshes Kern's humanity. Additionally, however, 'fraîcheur' carries associations of 'bloom', and Valentine, of course, with her beauty and innocence, is in the full rosy bloom of her youth.

18 Kieślowski's final film echoes Shakespeare's last play in several ways. Kern's secluded house is like an island; his study, with its books and surveillance equipment, recalls Prospero's library. Both film and play feature young lovers, shipwrecks, storms, 'magical' powers, and the theme of redemption through renunciation of asocial behaviour.

19 As Kieślowski explained wryly: 'We – or perhaps the judge – repaired that mistake in time which had been made, probably, by the one who is responsible for everything … but doesn't know everything.'

20 Stok, *Kieślowski on Kieślowski*, p. 79.

21 Ibid., pp. 134–5.

22 In this writer's opinion, Kieślowski's films also differ considerably from those of Europe's other 'spiritual' film-makers in terms of style. Dreyer and Bergman, particularly, tended to try to gain access to their characters' inner lives by means of frequent contemplation of the face in close-up, whereas the presence or otherwise of God might be suggested partly by moody evocations of architecture and landscape. The approach taken by Rossellini – certainly a Catholic film-maker, but less evidently 'spiritual' in his concerns than the other directors discussed here – was firmly aligned to his interest in observational 'realism', whereas Tarkovsky was a mystic whose slow, sometimes obscure narratives and near-static visual style seemed to demand a leap of faith on the part of the viewer. Perhaps Bresson comes closest to Kieślowski in his firmly materialist depiction of the world combined with a fascination with meaning derived from images being placed in context with one another. At the same time, however, his austere, pared-down visual style, his dislike of 'acting', and his Catholic emphasis on divine redemption and grace mark him as a very different artist from the Pole.

23 Intriguingly, although Kieślowski claimed that *White* also alluded to the fictional Dutch composer (Stok, *Kieślowski on Kieślowski*, p. 225), I have been able to find no such reference – verbal, musical or visual – in the finished film. One can, however, hear briefly in the background the tango from *White* during the record-store scene in *Red*.

24 Ibid., pp. 32–4; 194.

25 Ibid., pp. 210-11.

Credits

**TROIS COULEURS BLEU/
TRZY KOLORY NIEBIESKI/
THREE COLOURS BLUE**

France/Switzerland/Poland
1993

Copyright
MK2 Productions/CEO
Productions/France 3
Cinéma/CAB
Productions/"Tor"
Production
Production companies
MK2 Productions SA
(Paris)/CEO Productions
(Paris)/France 3 Cinéma
(Paris)/CAB Productions
(Lausanne)/"Tor" Production
(Warsaw)
With the participation of
Canal+
Supported by the Fonds
Eurimages of the Conseil de
l'Europe
With the participation of
Centre National de la
Cinématographie
A Marin Karmitz presentation
Producer
Marin Karmitz
Production manager
Yvon Crenn
**Unit managers/
administration**
Caroline Lassa, Aline
Corneille, Anne Guillemard,
Olivier Bulteau, Jean Talvat,
Nicolas Tempier,
Gisèle Vuillaume,
Dominique Lefevre

Director
Krzysztof Kieślowski
Assistant director
Emmanuel Finkiel
**Assistants to the
direction**
Julie Bertucelli, Stéphane
Libiot, Francois Azria,
Emmanuela Demarchi
Assistant to the director
Stan Latek
Script supervisor
Geneviève Dufour
Casting
Margot Capelier
Screenplay
Krzysztof Piesiewicz,
Krzysztof Kieślowski
Screenplay collaborators
Agnieszka Holland, Edward
Zebrowski, Slawomir Idziak
Dialogue translations
Marcin Latallo
Assistant translator
Roman Gren
Director of photography
Slawomir Idziak
Assistant operators
Henryk Jedynak, Muriel
Coulin
Stills/second camera
Piotr Jaxa
Grips
Albert Vasseur, Alain Dreze
Lighting
Hans Meier, Ernst Brunner,
Alain Dondin
Electrician
Alain Dubouloz
Editor
Jacques Witta

Assistant editors
Michele D'Attoma, Aïlo
Auguste, Catherine Cormon,
Urszula Lesiak
Art director
Claude Lenoir
Set decorators
Marie-Claire Quin, Jean-
Pierre Delettre, Christian
Aubenque, Julien Poitou-
Weber, Lionel Acat
Props
Michel Charvaz
Costumes
Virginie Viard, Naima
Lagrange
Make-up/hairdressers
Valerie Tranier, Jean-Pierre
Caminade
Titles/opticals
Ercidan
Music
Zbigniew Preisner
Music performed by
Warsaw Sinfonia (director
Wojciech Michniewski), The
Philharmonic Choir of Silesie
(choir master Jan Wojtacha)
Soprano:
Elzbieta Towarnika
Flute:
Jacek Ostaszewski
Piano:
Konrad Mastylo
**Executive music
producer**
Halina Laciak
Music engineers
Rafal Paczkowski
Assistant:
Leszek Kaminski

Sound
Jean-Claude Laureux
Sound recordists
Brigitte Taillandier, Pascal Colomb
Sound editors
Claire Bez, Bertrand Lenclos, Jean-Claude Laureux
Sound mixer
William Flageollet
Sound effects
Jean-Pierre Lelong, Mario Melchiorri, Vincent Arnardi
Press representatives
Eva Simonet
Assistant:
Laurette Monconduit

Juliette Binoche
Julie
Benoît Régent
Olivier
Florence Pernel
Sandrine
Charlotte Véry
Lucille
Hélène Vincent
Journalist
Philippe Volter
Estate agent
Claude Duneton
Doctor
Hugues Quester
Patrice
Emmanuelle Riva
Mother
Florence Vignon
Copyist
Jacek Ostaszewski
Flautist
Yann Tregouet
Antoine
Isabelle Sadoyan
Servant
Daniel Martin
Downstairs neighbour
Catherine Thérouenne
Neighbour
Alain Ollivier
Lawyer
Pierre Forget
Gardener
Philippe Manesse
Idit Cebula
Jacques Disses
Yves Penay
Arno Chevrier
Stanislas Nordey
Michel Lisowski
Philippe Morier-Genoud
Julie Delpy
Zbigniew Zamachowski
Alain Decaux

Dolby
In Colour
8,809 feet
98 minutes

**TROIS COULEURS BLANC/
TRZY KOLORY BIALY/
THREE COLOURS WHITE**

France/Switzerland/Poland
1993

Copyright
MK2 Productions/France 3
Cinéma/CAB Productions
S.A/"Tor" Production
Production companies
MK2 Productions SA/France
3 Cinéma /CAB Productions
S.A./"Tor" Production
With the participation of
Canal+
Supported by the Fonds
Eurimages of the Conseil de
l'Europe
A Marin Karmitz presentation
Producer
Marin Karmitz
Executive producer
Yvon Crenn
Production executives
"Tor" Studio:
Krzysztof Zanussi, Ryszard
Straszewski, Irena
Strzalkowska
Production manager
Ryszard Chutkowski
**Unit managers/
administration**
Krzysztof Staszewski,
Wlodzimierz Dziatkiewicz,
Joanna Pindelska, Andrzej
Buhl, Malgorzata Powalka,
Katarzyna Janus, Joanna
Kadubiec, Malgorzata
Witkowska, Caroline Lassa,
Anne Guillemard, Jean
Talvat, Gisele Vuillaume,
Aline Corneille, Olivier

Bulteau, Nicolas Tempier,
Dominique Lefevre
Director
Krzysztof Kieślowski
Assistant directors
Teresa Violetta Buhl,
Emmanuel Finkiel
**Assistants to the
direction**
Pawel Lozinski, Maria
Czartoryska, Adam
Paplinski, Peter Thurrell, Julie
Bertucelli, François Azria,
Stéphane Libiot
Assistant to the director
Stan Latek
Script supervisor
Geneviève Dufour
Casting
Margot Capelier, Teresa
Violetta Buhl
Screenplay
Krzysztof Piesiewicz,
Krzysztof Kieślowski
Screenplay consultants
Agnieszka Holland, Edward
Zebrowski, Edward Klosinski
Dialogue translations
Marcin Latallo
Assistant translator
Roman Gren
Director of photography
Edward Klosinski
Assistant operators
Henryk Jedynak, Muriel
Coulin
Stills
Piotr Jaxa
Grips
Zbigniew Koniuszy,
Stanislaw Kolenda, Albert
Vasseur, Alain Dreze
Lighting
Piotr Obloza, Sergiusz

Bogucki, Marek Socha,
Slawomir Grinka, Hans
Meier, Ernst Brunner, Alain
Dondin, Alain Dubouloz
Editor
Urszula Lesiak
Assistant editors
Ewa Lenkiewicz, Christian
Phan-Trong Tuan, Alicja
Torbus-Wosinska
Art directors
Halina Dobrowolska, Claude
Lenoir
Set decorator
Magdalena Dipont
Set dressers/props
Tomasz Kowalski, Dariusz
Lipinski, Henryk Puchalski,
Michel Charvaz, Julien
Poitou-Weber, Jean-Pierre
Delettre, Christian
Aubenque, Lionel Acat
Costumes
Elzbieta Radke, Teresa
Wardzala, Jolanta Luczak,
Virginie Viard
Make-up/hairdressers
Jolanta Pruszynska, Jadwiga
Cichocka, Jean-Pierre
Caminade
Titles/opticals
Ercidan
Music
Zbigniew Preisner
Music director
Zbigniew Paleta
Music performed by
Sextuor Cordes
Le petit orchestre de
Zbigniew Preisner
First Violin:
Zbigniew Paleta
Oboe:
Mariusz Pedzialek

THE 'THREE COLOURS' TRILOGY

Clarinet:
Jan Cielecki
Executive music producer
Halina Laciak, Preisner Production
Music engineers
Rafal Paczkowski
Assistant:
Leszek Kaminski
Music extract
"To ostatnia niedziela" by Jerzy Petersburski, Z. Friedwald
Sound
Jean-Claude Laureux
Sound recordists
Brigitte Taillandier, Pascal Colomb
Sound editors
Piotr Zawadzki, Jean-Claude Laureux, Francine Lemaitre
Sound mixer
William Flageollet
Sound effects
Jerome Levy, Pascal Maziere, Eric Ferret, Marc-Antoine Beldent
Stuntmen
Robert Brzezinski, Jozef Stefanski, Zbigniw Modej, Janusz Chlebowski, Ryszard Janikowski

Zbigniew Zamachowski
Karol Karol
Julie Delpy
Dominique Vidal
Janusz Gajos
Mikolaj
Jerzy Stuhr
Jurek
Grzegorz Warchol
Elegant man

Jerzy Nowak
Old peasant
Aleksander Bardini
Lawyer
Cezary Harasimowicz
Inspector
Jerzy Trela
Monsieur Bronek
Cezary Pazura
Bureau de change proprietor
Michel Lisowski
Interpreter
Piotr Machalica
Tall man
Barbara Dziekan
Cashier
Marzena Trybala
Mariott employee
Philippe Morier Genoud
Judge
Francis Coffinet
Bank employee
Yannick Evely
Metro employee
Jacques Disses
Dominique's lawyer
Teresa Budzisz Krzyzanowska
Madame Jadwiga
K. Bigelmajer
J. Dominik
J. Grzegorek
M. Kaczmarska
A. Kalinowski
S. Latek
J. Ladynska
M. Marciano
J. Mayzel
J. Modet
L. Okowity
A. Paplinski
W. Paszkowski
M. Prazmowska
M. Robaszkiewicz

Z. Richter
B. Szymanska
B. Topa
W. Wroblewska
M. Verner
P. Zelt
Juliette Binoche
Florence Pernel

Dolby
In Colour
8,275 feet
92 minutes

**TROIS COULEURS ROUGE/
TRZY KOLORY CZERWONY/
THREE COLOURS RED**

France/Switzerland/Poland
1994

Copyright
MK2 Productions S.A./
France 3 Cinéma/CAB
Productions S.A./"Tor"
Production
Production companies
MK2 Productions SA
(Paris)/France 3 Cinéma
(Paris)/CAB Productions SA
(Lausanne)/"Tor" Production
(Warsaw)
With the participation of
Canal+
Supported by the Fonds
Eurimages of the Conseil de
l'Europe
In co-production with the
Télévision Suisse Romande
(TSR) and with the support
of L'Office Fédéral de la
Culture Suisse du
Département Fédéral de
l'Interieur
A Marin Karmitz presentation
Producer
Marin Karmitz
Executive producer
Yvon Crenn
Production manager
Gérard Ruey
**Unit managers/
administration**
Heinz Dill, François Cesalli,
Xavier Grin, Blez Gabioud,
Olivier Zimmermann,
Christian Manzoni,
Nathalie Jaquinet,
Gisèle Vuillaume,
Christine Hulin, Hélène
Platel, Aline Corneille,
Florence Ruffetta,
Dominique Lefevre
Second unit
Stan Latek, Piotr Jaxa, Hans
Meier
Director
Krzysztof Kieślowski
Assistant director
Emmanuel Finkiel
**Assistants to the
Direction**
Thierry Mouquin, Pascal
Verdosci, Xavier Nicol, Jean-
Jacques Rossmann
Assistant to the director
Stan Latek
Script supervisor
Geneviève Dufour
Casting
Margot Capelier
Screenplay
Krzysztof Piesiewicz,
Krzysztof Kieślowski
Screenplay consultants
Agnieszka Holland, Edward
Zebrowski, Piotr Sobocinski
Dialogue translations
Marcin Latallo
Assistant translator
Roman Gren
Director of photography
Piotr Sobocinski
Camera operators
Steadicam:
Ricardo Brunner
Technocrane:
Martin C. Hume
Assistant operators
Henryk Jedynak, Muriel
Coulin
Stills/second camera
Piotr Jaxa
Grips
Albert Vasseur, Alain Dreze,
Bernard Weber
Chapman Apollo:
Roger Priot
Technocrane:
David Campbell
Lighting
Hans Meier, Salvatore
Piazzitta, Blaise Bauquis,
Eric André
Groupist
Alain Dubouloz
Editor
Jacques Witta
Assistant editors
Aïlo Auguste, Catherine
Cormon, Salvatore Di Meo,
Sandrine Normand, Bettina
Hoffmann, Urszula Lesiak,
Michele D'Attoma
Art director
Claude Lenoir
Set decorators/props
Daniel Mercier, Patrick Stoll,
David Stadelmann, Paola
Andreani, Pierre Agoston,
Patrick Flumet, Marc Babel,
Jean-François Despres,
Patrick Lehmann, Jean-
Pierre Balsiger, Michel
Charvaz, Yvan Niclass,
Markus Waldburger, Fabrice
Duplaissy, Vincent
Stadelmann, Jean-Paul
Trincat, Jean-Daniel Weber,
Philippe Brunisholz,
Guillaume Ogay
Costumes creations
Corinne Jorry

Costumes
Nadia Cuenoud, Véronique Michel
Fashion consultant
Christine Noussan
Make-up/hairdressers
Nathalie Tanner, Catherine Zingg
Titles/opticals
Ercidan
Music
Zbigniew Preisner
Additional:
Bertrand Lenclos
Zbigniew Preisner music performed by
Warsaw Sinfonia (conductor Wojciech Michniewski), The Philharmonic Choir of Silesie (choir master Jan Wojtacha)
Guitar:
Janusz Strobel
Cello:
Jerzy Klocek
Executive music producer
Halina Laciak, Preisner Production
Music engineers
Rafal Paczkowski
Assistant:
Leszek Kaminski
Van den Budenmayer music performed by
Orchestre Symphonique de Katowice (conductor Zdzislaw Szostak)
Soprano:
Elzbieta Towarnicka
Choreography
Brigitte Matteuzzi
Sound
Jean-Claude Laureux

Sound recordists
Brigitte Taillandier, Sandrine Henchoz
Sound editors
Piotr Zawadzki, Jean-Claude Laureux, Francine Lemaître, Nicolas Naegelen
Sound mixer
William Flageollet
Sound effects
Jean-Pierre Lelong, Mario Melchiorri, Vincent Arnardi
Press representative
Eva Simonet
Stunts
Lucien Abbet, Philippe Calame, Silvio Stoppa
Animal trainer
André Noël

Irène Jacob
Valentine Dussaut
Jean-Louis Trintignant
Judge Joseph Kern
Frédérique Feder
Karin
Jean-Pierre Lorit
Auguste Bruner
Samuel Lebihan
Photographer
Marion Stalens
Veterinary surgeon
Teco Celio
Barman
Bernard Escalon
Record dealer
Jean Schlegel
Neighbour
Elzbieta Jasinska
Woman
Paul Vermeulen
Karin's friend
Jean-Marie Daunas
Theatre manager

Roland Carey
Drug dealer
Brigitte Paul
Cecile Tanner
Leo Ramseyer
Anne Theurillat
Nader Farman
Neige Dolski
Jessica Korinek
Voice of Marc Autheman
Juliette Binoche
Julie Delpy
Benoît Régent
Zbigniew Zamachowski

Dolby
In Colour
8,934 feet
99 minutes

Bibliography

BOOKS
Bren, Frank, *World Cinema 1: Poland* (London: Flicks Books, 1986).
Butler, Ivan, *Religion in the Cinema* (London: Zwemmer, 1969).
Kieślowski, Krzysztof and Piesiewicz, Krzysztof (trans. Phil Cavendish and Susannah Bluh), *Decalogue: The Ten Commandments* (London: Faber and Faber, 1991).
Kieślowski, Krzysztof and Piesiewicz, Krzysztof (trans. Danusia Stok), *Three Colours Trilogy: Blue, White, Red* (London: Faber and Faber, 1998).
Michalek, Boleslaw and Turaj, Frank, *The Modern Cinema of Poland* (Bloomington: Indiana University Press, 1988).
Nowell-Smith, Geoffrey (ed.), *The Oxford History of World Cinema* (Oxford: Oxford University Press, 1996).
Schrader, Paul, *Transcendental Style in Film: Ozu, Bresson, Dreyer* (Berkeley: University of California Press, 1972).
Stok, Danusia (ed.), *Kieślowski on Kieślowski* (London: Faber and Faber, 1993).

SELECTED ARTICLES
Andrew, Geoff, 'True Blue', *Time Out* no. 1207, October 1993.
Andrew, Geoff, 'Giving Up the Ghost', *Time Out* no. 1262, October 1994.
Cavendish, Phil, 'Kieślowski's *Decalogue*', *Sight and Sound*, Summer 1990.
Rayns, Tony, 'Kieślowski: Crossing Over', *Sight and Sound*, March 1992.
Rayns, Tony, 'Glowing in the Dark', *Sight and Sound*, June 1994.

BFI MODERN CLASSICS

BFI Modern Classics is an exciting new series which combines careful research with high quality writing about contemporary cinema. Authors write on a film of their choice, making the case for its elevation to the status of classic. The series will grow into an influential and authoritative commentary on all that is best in the cinema of our time.

If you would like to receive further information about future **BFI Modern Classics** or about other books on film, media and popular culture from BFI Publishing, please fill in your name and address and return this card to the BFI*.

No stamp needed if posted in the UK, Channel Islands, or Isle of Man.

NAME

ADDRESS

POSTCODE

* North America: Please return your card to:
Indiana University Press, Attn: LPB, 601 N Morton Street,
Bloomington, IN 47401-3797

BFI Publishing
21 Stephen Street
FREEPOST 7
LONDON
W1E 4AN